CALIFORNIA CONTINUUM

VOLUME 1:
MIGRATIONS AND AMALGAMATIONS

GRANT HIER
&
JOHN BRANTINGHAM

California Continuum, Volume 1: Migrations and Amalgamations
by Grant Hier and John Brantingham

ISBN: 978-1-938349-81-2

eISBN: 978-1-938349-97-3

Copyright © 2019 Grant Hier and John Brantingham

This work is licensed under the Creative Commons Attribution-NonCommercial-NoDerivatives 4.0 International License. To view a copy of this license, visit http://creativecommons.org/licenses/by-nc-nd/4.0/.

Front cover photograph "DETRITAL SEDIMENTARY ROCK" by Grant Hier.

Back cover photograph "ISS View of the Southwestern USA" by NASA Earth Observatory (public domain). The long and narrow blue patch bleeding off the bottom edge (center) is the Salton Sea, and the smaller blue oval of the same color near the top (above the word POETS and just below the banner) is Mono Lake. To the left of Mono Lake, the dark Sierra Nevada range (lined in white clouds) runs halfway down the image. To the left of that is California's Central Valley (long green patch) with the Pacific Ocean beyond (westward). Las Vegas is the pale green patch centered below the two central cloud patches. Below that and slightly to the right is the dark blue-green of Lake Mead and Hoover Dam. The Grand Canyon and Colorado River can be seen at the far lower right (and extending above the bar code).

Layout and book design by Mark Givens and Grant Hier

First Pelekinesis Printing 2019

For information:
Pelekinesis, 112 Harvard Ave #65, Claremont, CA 91711 USA

Excerpt from "California, Calafia, Khalif: The Origin of the Name 'California'" by Robert Petersen, KCET Departures Copyright © KCETLink, 2015. Used with permission.

Library of Congress Cataloging-in-Publication Data

Names: Hier, Grant, author. | Brantingham, John, author.
Title: California continuum.
Description: Claremont, CA : Pelekinesis, [2018]- | Includes bibliographical references and index.
Identifiers: LCCN 2018042787 (print) | LCCN 2019002434 (ebook) | ISBN 9781938349973 (ePub) | ISBN 9781938349812 (paperback)
Subjects: LCSH: California--Literary collections.
Classification: LCC PS571.C2 (ebook) | LCC PS571.C2 C145 2018 (print) | DDC 810.8/09794--dc23
LC record available at https://lccn.loc.gov/2018042787

www.pelekinesis.com

VOLUME I:
MIGRATIONS AND AMALGAMATIONS

GRANT HIER

&

JOHN BRANTINGHAM

For Laura

And for Annie

CONTENTS

Preface by Robert Petersen 13
Introduction by D. J. Waldie 15
Foreword by Grant Hier 21
Foreword by John Brantingham 33

Part One: Go to the West

For Those of You Who Don't Understand, That's What You
    Call Real Love 39
1850 44
Continental Drift 45
Nathaniel 46
The Bones 47
The Balance of the Table 48
South-Western Migration 49
Art in the West 50
Signal Hill 51
Layers 52
Lots 53
The Three Strikes Rule 56
The Savior 59

Part Two: Symbols of Human Failure

The Golden Gate Bridge 65
In the Tule Fog 66
All of Those Boys Are Dead Now 68
As the City Burns 77
Post-War 79
The Bombing of Goleta 80
Zoot Suit Riots 81
We'll Be Thinking of You 82
The View from Porcupine Hill 86
Ringtailed Dreams 89
The View from Signal Hill 90

Part Three: I Am Not Free

Sandra Who 97
The Sorrowful Music of Cows 98
The Fountainhead 101
Fight or Flight 102
Captured 104
Marty Was Here 106
The Last Day of March 110
A Kind of Social Justice 111
A Quick Moment of Tom 116
Square Nails 122
Allison 123
Martha Who 124

Part Four: A Thinking Animal

The Water Hunter 129
Acts of Self-Destruction.. 132
The Train Whistle 136
The World Gone to Flame.. 137
Buffalo Soldiers... 141
The Killer of Men, The Killer of Trees 142
"Remember when we get there, honey..." 145
Ferdinand, Lincoln, McKinley.. 147
Lily Liver... 149

Part Five: A Single Thing In Nature

No Socks 157
In the Land of Drought.. 176
Daughter of the Mammoth Hunter 179
In The Land Of Bears 180
The California Water War.. 191
Halcyon Solstice... 193
Tannerite... 194
Disheveled 196
Smelling March.. 201
The San Francisco Earthquake, 1906...................................... 202
Eureka 205
Internal Injuries 207
Praising Strange Gods 213

Part Six: Driving Wedges

Howard's Magic 217
The Beauty of a Bettie Page Haircut 221
The Snake 226
Marathon Man 228
The View from the Monkey Bars 230
Broken Bones 231
The Last Hope for Doris Day 232
When Rachel Sleeps 236
Children Let Your Voices Sing Higher Than the Explosions 237
E Pluribus Unum 241

Notes 247
Acknowledgments 249
About The Authors 252

PREFACE

CALIFORNIA HAS psychologically come to represent a land of promise, possibility, and opportunity... But even though the name "California" is known throughout the world, most people, including its own residents, are unaware of the origin of its name... The name "California" derives from a 16th Century romance novel written by a Spanish author named García Ordóñez de Montalvo... The novel described an island, very close to the Garden of Eden, full of gold, which was ruled by strong and beautiful black women... Spanish explorers during the 1500s were familiar with the story and applied the name to what is now called Baja California [and] once the name started being used on maps, it stuck... The inspiration for the word was likely "Khalif" or "Khalifa" which means "successor" in Arabic... The Islamic origin of the name illustrates an example of how our lives are affected by many different cultural influences, even if we are not explicitly aware of them. In addition to coffee, algebra, hospitals, and toothbrushes, the name of our state finds its origin in the Muslim world. Just like our present day state, the name "California" is a confluence of multiple cultural influences... So the name "California" traces its origin to a centuries old story about an island, full of gold, run by black women who fed men to their pet griffins. Like other Amazonian legends, the island of California was a place filled with strong, self-sufficient women who solicited male attention completely on their own terms. This story resonates in California, which has a long history of gender roles being reconstructed. And it is fitting that this state, which has served as a frontier for issues of race, gender and religion, gets its name from a mythical story where race, gender and religion collide. Finally, the story of an island full of gold foreshadowed the Gold Rush, which propelled the idea of the California dream around the world.

This state, which has spawned so many of its own myths, has its origin in myth. The Spanish explorers were looking for an "island dream" when they gave California its name. And hundreds of years later, people still come to California searching for their own piece of the California dream.

— From "California, Calafia, Khalif: The Origin of the Name 'California'" by Robert Petersen

INTRODUCTION

D. J. WALDIE

§

A FEELING FOR HISTORY

This collection—expected to be the first in a series—is the collaborative work of poets John Brantingham and Grant Hier. Their forewords here position their micro-narratives—branching, overlapping, circulating—as enactments of connections and displacements through 13,000 years of California history. They are intended to evoke the felt sense of something happening. As a set of provocations, they drive a narrative that is generative of the way the passing of time is experienced. They perform the intensity and resonance that make the past habitable, but without the enclosure of a novel's interiority or the curated and assigned correspondences of an academic study. The narrative form is "rhizomatic," and like a fleshy root, it ramifies below the surface to effloresce *ad libitum* as points of impact and reaction, of contingencies and emergences, of trajectories commencing and dead ends reached. Assembled here as "sudden" stories, freely fictional, these presences, in time and of time, make palpable the touch of several Californian pasts—of pasts that are true enough, of pasts seeking un-preconceived for what ought to be true, and of some that are true because they are too beautiful or terrible not to be.

California has too often been misplaced within the dichotomy of too beautiful Eden (respite, health, youth, liberation) and too terrible Donner Pass[1] (abandonment, loss, defilement, rot). The abstraction of those master narratives of California—boosterism on one side of the coin, fear on the other side—leaves little room for the intimate and local knowledges generated by the rhythms of daily life and the patterns in remembrance, ritual, and habit. Local knowledges (always in relation to major events and their contexts) are never more than tentative but never less than charged with barely contained intensities, pluripotent in effect, and lived. They are filtered, refined, and repurposed dialogically through generational narratives and communal memory (not without risk of inherited bias and cultural phobias). In their attunements, textures, and atmospheres, local knowledges resist erasure. In place of the frictionless efficiency of the world's regime of speed, they substitute rumination and speculation, particularity and partiality, fusions and confusions. Worlds are unfolded there for the subjective observer-participant, worlds available for inhabitation through lore and daydream, as something imagined but not uncritically. "To remain in touch with the past requires a love of memory," wrote Gaston Bachelard, the philosopher of sensuous remembering. "To remain in touch with the past requires a constant imaginative effort."[2] This sensibility is a kind of intelligence about the world, emergent in interleavings, immanent in specifics, and poetic in expression. In its reluctance to give the obvious interpretation to events, in its

---

1   To be Californian required belief in a myth of blind luck—the Gold Rush and the exuberant binge that followed. But the myth has a monstrous alternative. It's the story of the Donner Party's snowbound wagon train and the cannibalism in Donner Pass that followed. There have been times when just surviving California is a kind of success.

2   Gaston Bachelard, "A Retrospective Glance at the Lifework of a Maker of Books," Fragments of a Poetics of Fire.

readiness to remain mystified, it seeks to drag things into view that actually feel like something³.

In his forward, Grant Hier imagines "the history surrounding (a) single item, the connections to the past we might discover were we able to learn the details of its days: what the land...beneath it looked like, what the words spoken by its owner sounded like, what day-to-day life was like for all those who laid eyes upon it." The potency that a "single item" has wound within it, a capacity to affect and to be affected, gives the history embodied in the stories in this collection the quality of continuous epiphanies that enmesh the local, the regional, and the global. The "single item" is a brick in "For Those of You Who Don't Understand, That's What You Call Real Love" and its touch is a blow that shatters Reginald Denny's skull at the start of the 1992 Los Angeles riots. Other items appear (and sometimes reappear)—a corpse, a quantity of ammonal explosive, a Native American "cogged stone," a deer, a bone, a fragment of glazed pottery—to instigate recursive histories whose interest (and risk) is not in fixing what California means but apprehending where everyday life in California has been going. Becoming Californian is an unfinished crossing. Its terminus might be the disaster of Donner Pass rather than the lucky accident of El Dorado. The stories assembled as *Migrations and Amalgamations* might be thought of as wayfinders in contested territory, needing Brantingham and Hier as indigenous guides and the pilgrim's wary trust, along with a measure of humility, a capacity for dialog, a tolerance for puzzlement, a suspension of assumptions, and deference to local customs.

Californians have to become vulnerable to their place at the same time they struggle to endure it.⁴ They "must awaken the

---

3   "... (W)orlds of all kinds that catch people up in *some*thing that feels like something." Kathleen Stewart, *Ordinary Affects*.

4   "(Y)ou have to cherish the world at the same time that you struggle to endure it," Flannery O'Connor, *The Habit of Being: Letters of Flannery O'Connor*.

stories that sleep in the streets and that sometimes lie within a simple name."⁵ The stories in this collection rise from sleeping in the streets, along with the homeless of Los Angeles. They take a simple name—Jésus—and make it not so simple. They take blows and give them, because the "single item" in many of these stories is a violent man. They trespass borders, police containment areas, and historical eras. They describe ecologies of the vernacular and map habitats of memory. These stories—untheorized, elliptical, spectral—pile up shadows and traces of sites of real damage and sometimes of real hope. They pierce the torpor of clichéd narratives of California to bleed through as if the stories themselves knew how much Californians needed them. Not for the clarity of their answers, but for the texture of knowing they embody. Not because they are suppressed stories from below, but because they are the as-yet-unexpressed stories from all around. (Readers should look forward to additional micro-narratives and their diverse narrators as the *California Continuum* series expands.)

The stories ahead stage the circulation and transformation of things that cannot be predicted or fully defined. They draw their force from discerning the resonances that linger in familiar scenes, commonplace relationships, and ordinary manifestations, steadily picking up density and texture as they move through time. The imaginative apprehension of the immanent in the everyday makes a habit of watching for something to happen that actually "feels like something" in a relay of correspondences that spark astonishment, enchantment, or consolation until everything at hand becomes "charged, overwhelming, and alive."⁶

The materials of the commonplace are the much handled things of living. They are touched and return a touch. Being touched

---

5 "Living is narrativizing. Stirring up or restoring this narrativizing is thus among the tasks of any renovation. One must awaken the stories that sleep in the streets...." Michel de Certeau, *The Practice of Everyday Life, Vol. 2, Living and Cooking.*

6 Stewart, *Ordinary Affects.*

and touching should have outcomes that are "political" (a sympathetic bond between strangers) and "cultural" (a sense of place that maps an inner landscape of recollection on the external contours of the familiar). Ordinary practices, so embodied, aim to activate a moral imagination—an imagination capable of dwelling in someone else's experience—that is in "constant contact and interchange between the local scene and the wide world that lies beyond it."[7]

Californians, because of the way in which their place became Joan Didion's "wearying enigma," suffer a hunger of memory as familiar to them as a coyote standing watchfully in the middle of a suburban street or a wildfire burning along a ridgeline. Californians hope that their place will reveal itself, that California will stop escaping their grasp, stop turning into something else, something that may be feral or not, redeeming or not. It's never very clear, because Californians are inheritors of a malign tradition in which—as fable, satire, or diatribe—their place is without a usable past, a viable present, or a future anyone would want. This rendering of California has been just another burlesque best witnessed while lightly sedated. To come alive to their place, Californians need new stories and habits of being. They need a feeling for history. It will reveal itself, as the stories in this collection seek to do, in sharing local knowledges and handing them on to current neighbors and to the future, where other Californians, in their myriad identities, wait to hear them.

— D. J. Waldie
Lakewood, California
2018

---

7 Lewis Mumford, *The South in Architecture*.

FOREWORD
GRANT HIER

§

OF FLASH FLOODS, FLAMING THREADS, AND THE BLANKET OF HISTORY

GERONIMO'S HORSE blanket. Imagine the history surrounding that single item, the connections to the past we might discover were we able to learn the details of its days: what the land that passed beneath it looked like, what the words spoken by its owner sounded like, what day-to-day life was like for all those who laid eyes upon it. The "History" that we are taught in schools and books most often focuses on the most extraordinary individuals and incidents of change, presented as linear narrative threads, highlighted as separate from the whole cloth. But history is not a singular thread or fabric, not a river of ink or a flood. Rather, it immerses all in the here and now and seeps vertically down through the past—cascading through time and touching all who ever lived. And it's not just about the extraordinary. The world is shaped by all of us, one person at a time, one gesture at a time—both the small and the large, the ordinary and extraordinary. The totality of it is our true history. All of it.

Yet only an infinitesimal bit of history ever gets written down, and that "Recorded History" is terribly selective and inexact. Like digging up a few bones—a shard of joint, claw, and skull—and assembling from that an approximation of what the beast looked like, then filing that away as reality. Actually, it is more like briefly glimpsing someone else's approximation from the shards they dug up or studied, and adopting that as our own understanding of things. Single narratives are told to us in isolation, starting with family mythologies handed down by elders. The societal "Official History" is gained through brief glimpses of the pre-assembled skeletons presented through the biases of scholars and writers, often amplified in the interest of the power structures of the storytellers, who themselves have reformed bits and pieces from extant archives (of subjective and biased reporting, diaries, societal myths and so on) into re-imagined digestible narratives for us, employing artistic license and educated guesses to augment, to fill in the gaps, to provide a singular context. Which is still, at its best, a museum skeleton that is mostly plastic fill-in, not actual bone, and not at all like the full reality that was.

Now consider the fact that we have glimpsed only a very small percentage of those grossly incomplete histories that others have dug up and reconstructed—those that are both written in a language we can comprehend and that are accessible to us. Yet these selective and inexact creative reproductions of the past become our official record of what happened, and what we accept as the "True History" of things in our minds. Well, that which we can manage to remember, of course. Consider this unsettling fact: the latest neuroscientific research tells us that each memory we have gets reconstructed anew and altered a bit each time we recall it, so we are not remembering the original input whenever we think of it, we are remembering the last version stored, which has been altered at each access before re-storing—like a distorted Xerox of a Xerox of a Xerox, re-personalized, re-colored, and revised by others' comments and our own imaginations and cognitive dissonances and secret wishes of the psyche.

Even our personal experiences get fictionalized throughout our lives with each recollection. Empirical shards get stored and reassembled and distorted by each separate creature in isolation. A few of our assembled narratives get handed off to be distorted by others. Meanwhile, all of existence is. And was.

§

Geronimo's horse blanket, one of the few personal possessions of the legendary Apache warrior, was most likely taken from him in 1886 when he surrendered to government troops, perhaps while it was still draped across his horse. It eventually ended up in the hands of the Sheriff of Los Angeles County, Martin G. Aguirre, who himself had a legacy for capturing bandits and "enemies of the state." Aguirre later became a very close friend of my father's mother and father, Hilda Elizabeth Hier and George Richard Hier. As the best man at their wedding, Aguirre was in his sixties, a lifelong bachelor with no descendants, so perhaps this contributed to his willingness to give my grandparents one of his prized possession as a wedding gift.

Aguirre himself was a lifelong horse man, the last Los Angeles Sheriff to patrol on horseback, so it would make sense that he would have specific interest in owning that famous item. As a boy, Aguirre would ride as volunteer with the local firefighters. William A. Hammel, his childhood and lifelong friend (and later an L.A. Sheriff as well) told a reporter that Martin Aguirre "had a little roan pony which could run like a jackrabbit. At the sound of the alarm he used to throw himself onto the roan pony and come tearing across the fields to the fire house, swinging his lasso as he came. When he got to the fire house he would lasso the end of the hose wagon and tear off down the rutty roads with the thing bounding and bouncing along in the trail of the pony." (Otherwise, the hose wagon would have had to be pulled to the fire by hand.) As a young man Aguirre rode herd with the cattle on the large estates between Los Angeles and Long Beach. As a 27 year-old Deputy, Aguirre's masterful riding skills came into play during "The Great Flood of 1886" when, after prolonged rains, the Los Angeles River suddenly overflowed its banks, taking the levees with it. *The Los Angeles Herald* reported: "Early that Monday evening the water came down in one continuous sheet from the top of the Sierras... people thought but little of the danger of a flood until about 2 o'clock Tuesday morning, when the officers who were patrolling along the river saw the water begin to rise quite rapidly. Others, as Deputy Sheriff Martin Aguirre, who lives a mile down Alameda street...were startled by the river invading their bedrooms. The police...and the awakened citizens gave the alarm and those in danger began to move out at once. An hour or two later the water came in a tidal wave...rolling waves seven feet high and carrying great boulders and tall pine trees in an indescribable ruin along its victorious path...bridges were swept from their abutments, iron structures of great strength being hurled along the torrents and their component parts broken to pieces. The iron rails were twisted like corkscrews by the mad swirl of waters and the fastening bolts snapped asunder as if the wrought iron were rotten wood.... While attempting to rescue others from drowning, Martin Aguirre was washed off his horse, the animal rolling him over in the current while attempting to bring little Teresa Whitney ashore. He was carried a mile down stream before he could make the land. He had a severe hemorrhage after this mishap."

Despite the surprising poetry in this newspaper account, the dramatic subject matter and the great importance of the event in Los Angeles at the time, I would imagine very few people alive today knew that L.A. had such a flood in 1886. Much less that the rivers of Southern California, up until a generation ago, often flooded their banks (why the Tongva made their "wikiup" reed houses moveable).

And even after just reading about that history of the flood, rich details of the human drama that occurred had been omitted. The L.A. County Sheriff archives account included this: "Deputy Aguirre attempted his last rescue where First Street ran into the river. He swam out and pulled Mrs. Whitney's little girl, Theresa, from the window of her house." A different newspaper story added more details: "He was an expert horseman, and all in one night in February he rode warning people down along Center Street. By morning houses and sheds were being washed down the torrential stream. Time and again he rode into the roaring flood and took out men, women and children until he had saved the lives of nineteen persons."

So the added details make the amazing story even more amazing, the acts of courage even more remarkable: Aguirre pulled little Theresa Whitney from the window of her home, yes, but it happened as that house was careening down the middle of the river. And even with this added color, more compelling details of that night are to be discovered, some of it sounding like a fabricated Comic Book Superhero plotline. One newspaper reporter wrote: "Martin told me that just as the flood waters came tearing down the river bed, two blazing meteors fell, one struck near Long Beach; the other was never found. He was standing near the flooded river watching these meteors when the water came down with an appalling rush. Houses came floating past with people on the roofs and screaming from the windows, all crying for help. Martin had a fine saddle horse in a livery stable on Aliso street. He ran for his horse and came back to the river on a dead run. Without hesitation, he headed his horse for the flood and plunged in. They fought their way to one of the houses. Martin seized a woman in his arms and turned his horse back to the bank. Nineteen times he made the plunge and nineteen times fought his way back through the flood. The last time he picked a little girl out from the window of a house that was rushing and careening by in the flood. By this time he was terribly exhausted and he could feel the horse weakening underneath him. He had gone into the raging torrents for the first time at First Street; his last trip was made where Seventh Street now crosses the river. As they struggled back to the bank—both he and the horse at the end of their strength—they struck a half submerged picket fence. The horse fell and turned over and over in the water as he was flung downstream. Martin had just time to throw the child onto the fence as he was torn from the saddle and tumbled over by the waters. He managed to right himself and—an inch at a time—swam back to the fence where he had left the child. She was gone. To the day of his death, he could never tell that story without emotion. There was always an ache in his heart for the little girl he failed to save."

It is here that we find the heart of history (regardless of whether some of this was exaggerated or mythologized after the fact), and this is precisely the driving force behind the writing in this book. In locating heroic acts and emotional truths within our day-to-day survival—the human gestures that reveal our courage as we risk to care for each other and to forgive, as we struggle to connect and hold on however we can as the world overwhelms us, and how our existence depends upon it—we discover an emotional continuum, we discern where the tapestry of humanity is reinforced. Beyond any headline or history book chapter heading, this is the weave that connects our personal history to others, in the moment-by-moment acts that define our character and our caring—individually, and cumulatively as a community. It is nothing short of the entirety of the species that creates our history one gesture at a time, yet over time we forget the streaking meteors, the exhausted man and horse tumbling underwater in turbulent muddy chaos at dawn, the regret we carry in our most private hours.

The Mayor made a public proclamation of Aguirre's "daring

bravery," and the Los Angeles County Bar Association recognized Deputy Aguirre's "bravery and valor" as they "presented him with a gold watch, a prized possession which he always carried with him." He was also given a Remington six-shot revolver that used to belong to a condemned murderer, a gift of the Sheriff of Los Angeles at the time, George E. Gard, who recruited Aguirre to be his Deputy. The year was 1886—the same year that Geronimo surrendered.

§

Three years after his heroic acts during the flood, Aguirre would become the first Latino Sheriff of Los Angeles County, often patrolling on horseback, sometimes riding his horse through the San Gabriel mountain range to the north of the old Pueblo of Los Angeles—the same range that my grandfather and grandmother would later homestead on, on the other side of the ridge.

My grandparents would work and live in Los Angeles during the week, then strap a mattress, lumber, tools and supplies to the back of a stake-bed truck, and drive the Sierra Highway past Vasquez Rocks to the foothills of Littlerock in the Antelope Valley, and there they would spend the weekend building their cabin home by hand. At night they would sleep in the open air on the mattress on the truck bed, marveling at the clarity of the stars and the river of the Milky Way arcing horizon-to-horizon over their heads. It was here, in the wild unclaimed lands of California, that they were to dig wells, erect windmills, drag roads, string fences, sew seeds of wheat and alfalfa—and by so improving the land, Los Angeles County granted them the deed to that land. Homesteading, it was called, and much of California was developed this way, up and down the state. My grandparents later built a second home nearby, on the floor of the western Mojave that nestled against the foothills, the high desert just off Fort Tejon Road. My grandfather hand-painted and hung a sign at the gate: Hier-View Ranch.

Throughout my childhood, my sister Suzan and I would spend weekends up at The Ranch, as we called it—although the name "ranch" might be misleading. Really, it was just a few acres of Mojave cleared of the Joshua tree, Juniper, yucca, Mexican sage and creosote, the perimeter defined by a three-strand barbed-wire fence protecting a small home, garage, and a metal windmill creaking in the breeze, drawing cold water up from deep under the hot sand. In the high desert, even after the hottest days, the nights could get so cold it stung your cheeks, and it would sometimes snow in the winter. With the San Gabriel foothills only a few hundred yards to the south, we had a red wooden sled with our names painted on it, kept up in the rafters of the garage. Right next to a stinky old blanket. Too stinky to hang in the house, apparently. And so, by the time I was born, Geronimo's personal horse blanket had spent decades in storage in the garage at Hier-View Ranch. I think my grandfather had said it stunk because it was wool. This was the blanket Geronimo sometimes wore over his shoulders to warm him and to keep him dry (it was woven so tight, it was waterproof), and he placed it across the back of his horse when he rode. So perhaps part of what I smelled had been the essence of Geronimo's own sweat, with the sweat of his horse mixed in there too. At the time, I had (still have) a 1959 book titled *Indian Chiefs*, and one of the chapters is all about Geronimo, with duo-tone illustrations of him rendered in orange and black. One drawing depicts him riding his horse full tilt, leaning over its neck, a blanket under him with no saddle. As a child, I would imagine the man in the book sitting on the blanket in the garage.

§

This brings us back to the original point, that history books are grossly incomplete and inaccurate. Geronimo's grandfather had been a chief, but Geronimo himself was not, despite the many sources (including my *Indian Chiefs* book) that claimed he was. Geronimo was a Medicine Man, married at 17, had nine wives and three children. When he was 21, and traveling into town with other men to trade for supplies, his camp was attacked by 400 Mexican soldiers. They killed his wife, his children, and his mother. From then on, it is claimed that Geronimo hated Mexicans and would attack almost any he encountered. He organized forces against all invaders. Dozens of Apaches accompanied him and followed his orders, so he was certainly a warrior and a leader—but he was never a tribal chief. As the Apache-U.S. conflict progressed, Geronimo surrendered three separate times within a 10-year period, breaking out of confinement each time. His fourth and final surrender in 1886, after a long pursuit in Mexico, made him the last Native American warrior to surrender to the U.S. government at the end of the plains wars.

Because of our limited understanding of history, few realize Geronimo spent the last third of his life as a homesick prisoner of war and an exploited tourist attraction. At first, people paid to parade past him in his cell at whatever fort he was being held in, and when being transported, passengers on the train would pay 25 cents a pop to cut buttons off his shirt. (At depot stops, more buttons were purchased and sewn back on for future passengers along the way.) Geronimo learned to print his name in block letters, and was allowed to sell his signature on items to earn income (although the government took most of the cut of each sale). Eventually, as the details of "The Apache Wars" spread via newspaper accounts, he became notorious, and so he was exploited even more for profit. The Omaha Exposition was the first to bill him as a headline attraction, and when the public swarmed to see the historic legend in the flesh, he started being loaned out to fairs and expositions where he would stand on display in Apache clothing, flanked by U.S. Army guards, and pose for souvenir photographs. In "Pawnee Bill's Wild West Show," spectators once again paid money to cut buttons off the once "bloodthirsty" but now "tamed" Apache "chief." Toward the end of his life, reporters would travel to interview the last "American Indian Chief" to be captured. Folklore grew that Geronimo's horse blanket had been made of the scalps of people he killed in battle, but when journalists asked him about it, they were disappointed when he insisted that there was never any such scalp blanket, although he did once own a personal horse blanket.

The blanket we had sure stunk, but I doubt it was because of human flesh.

Whatever it was, desert rats found it interesting enough to nibble on over the years, but not interesting enough to devour entirely. One day, perhaps on a December morning when we were pulling down the sled, my grandfather decided the blanket wasn't worth anything anymore because of the holes and frayed edges, and so he heaved it into his incinerator—a large yellow-orange oil drum with holes in the side to vent the flames, what desert dwellers employed to get rid of their garbage and trash. And so it was that the once-living-sheep-wool-turned-to-horse-blanket owned by the once-living-Apache-Medicine-Man-turned-warrior-turned-to-exploited-prisoner vanished from history, lifting up as black smoke and ash to become part of the sands and sky of the California desert basin, just north of Los Angeles, sometime in the mid-1960s, some 80 years after Geronimo last held it in his hands. Discarded, and all but forgotten. Until now, where the story rests in your hands. (Or rather, a reassembled narrative of it.)

I used to joke that the perceived family I.Q. diminishes whenever that blanket-burning story is disclosed. On the PBS program *Antiques Roadshow*, a Navaho blanket from around 1850 received the highest estimated value in the history of the show: $350,000 - $500,000. Someone watching that episode decided to get his own blanket appraised, even though he thought it was worthless, and it proved to be authentic and sold at auction for $1.5 million. I can only imagine what Geronimo's personal horse blanket would be worth today had it survived, even with frayed edges and holes.

Rather than rue what might have been, the value of that blanket still exists, at least, in realizing how painful it is to ignore our connections to the past, the richness of what came before, and what it might teach us today. Beyond that, there's a greater consideration that has yet been acknowledged: the ignorance of historical narratives that are all-too-first-person to the point of myopia. As in life, when we view events with ourselves at the center, with everything happening to us and revolving around us, we lack the perspective of others' experiences and of our place in the whole. This makes for biased and incomplete versions of history—as when I might ask you to feel remorse that our family's blanket was lost, say, when in fact it really wasn't ours to begin with, and when the cultural meaning of it was never fully appreciated by its secondary and tertiary owners. But if we can instead imagine the backstory of that warrior's grief as he returns home to discover that his wife, children, mother, and entire community has been massacred, if we can empathize with the Medicine Man as the last of his world is being invaded by violent intruders, as he is captured and stripped of his possessions and pride, mocked and exploited while he ages in a cage and drowns in homesickness in his final decades, then that blanket of history can be seen in a whole new light.

That is the goal of this book, then, unique in its approach. The imagined interior lives of those standing just outside of the frame of what has been recorded as "True History." All attempted fictional histories run the risk of misrepresenting the past, and sometimes grossly (see *Gone with the Wind*). Still, if we can seek the humanity lost to the shadows, as John and I do here, then we might discover a deeper understanding of our past, one that traditional history books have failed to reach.

Call it what you will—Flash Fiction, Hint Fiction, Micro-Fiction, Sudden Fiction, Short-Shorts—these are highly compressed stories which might seem at first as unrelated, non-linear narratives, but which are interconnected in many ways: via common natural forces that cut across the character's lives (water, fire, etc.); via common structures (towers, bridges, holes, etc.); via common themes (migration, reconstruction, redemption); by locations visited centuries (or even thousands of years) apart; by common objects touched; by shared emotional truths, and more. The similarity across time between simple daily acts of grace and dishonor, of charity and indecency, in the daily struggle of our existence. The emotional truths that connect our lives to everyone, not just those here with us now, but all those who came before us.

— Grant Hier
    Anaheim, 2018

FOREWORD

JOHN BRANTINGHAM

I woke up in a Chicago Best Western to find the ghost of John Steinbeck sitting on a chair at the window lighting a cigarette. I was in Chicago away from California for the Association of Writers and Writing Programs Conference in 2012 or it could have been 2013 or 2011. It's hard to keep history straight.

It was my fault he was here. I had summoned him the night before in a long conversation about my changing relationship with his work. Years before, I had written the first draft of a master's thesis that I never turned in about the nature of religion in his writing.

He's a hard one to nail down. I had spent my twenties idolizing him. Now in my forties, I had started to reread him only to find that like many writers, he was human. I found racism, sexism, and homophobia where I had not seen it before. I found faulty logic. I found stereotype.

I also found all the beauty that I had seen there before and a man who had been trying, really and truly trying, to be a good person, and he had succeeded in that many, many times. I sat up in bed and watched him watching me. He smoked his cigarette and sipped his coffee, and in his eyes, I saw his thoughts. He was thinking, "All right then. If you know so much, do better."

That's a hell of a kind of order coming from the master.

Hands in his pockets, Steinbeck followed about ten paces behind me around Chicago that day, to the conference and beyond. That's when I met Grant again outside the hotel. I hadn't really seen him since the late nineties when we were in college together. Facebook had kept us in touch. We'd emailed. He'd been working on an epic poem about the natural world of Los Angeles for a long time. What I knew about Grant in the years since I'd seen him was that we'd both been working on the same themes from different directions. Yes, it was nature, but it was something more.

We'd both been wrestling with what California is. It's a big kind of question, one that probably can't be answered. Steinbeck tried but gave us only a piece of it and one that came through a lens I didn't like.

Grant nodded at the apparition behind me. "What's with Steinbeck?"

I shrugged, suddenly a sullen teenager again. "You ever read 'Breakfast'?"

"His short story?"

"Yeah," I said. Steinbeck was smoking again. I had the feeling he was itching for some wine. "It's maybe the best thing he ever wrote. Sometimes I think it's most beautiful short story ever written."

"That's a bold statement."

"It's short, just over a thousand words, but he digs into the world like I've never seen anywhere else in his work. It speaks the truth about California. Just a bit of it, but it's real. *East of Eden* is fine, and it's gigantic, and it just doesn't have the dramatic power of his microfiction."

Grant cocked his head and stared at Steinbeck for a moment. "Well," he said. "I guess that's probably the key to it."

Steinbeck shifted his weight back to one heel and regarded Grant with a shock of revelation in his eyes.

That's how this book started. I have no illusions about besting the master, but I do hope there is some truth.

— John Brantingham
Wolverton, Sequoia and Kings Canyon
National Parks, 2018

PART ONE
GO TO THE WEST

"If any young man is about to commence the world, we say to him, publicly and privately, Go to the West."

— Horace Greeley

FOR THOSE OF YOU WHO DON'T UNDERSTAND, THAT'S WHAT YOU CALL REAL LOVE

THE IRON oxide came from red veins in a cliff rimming a desert box canyon. Its younger rust cousins, in miniature, lined the parallel welded seams of the truck that had hauled it away. Some of that transported ore was split off, processed, hauled in rustless trucks, and sold in tubes of burnt sienna and burnt umber oil paints. Several months later, coincidentally, bits of the original cliff would be reunited on the vertical plane of a gessoed canvas as those oil paints were spread by a fine paintbrush made of red hairs taken from the tail of a wild male weasel from Siberia mixed with hairs taken from the ear of an ox from northeast China (but sold via mail order as brush made of kolinsky sable-hair), and that original painting was hung in a gallery on La Brea, then sold to hang on a black and white striped entryway wall of a beach house in Malibu Colony.

Meanwhile, in the Crestmore quarry of Riverside, between the 10 and 60 Freeways on Rubidoux Boulevard just south of Fontana, metamorphic rocks were blasted and scraped to separate the lime and magnesia that had clung fast for centuries. That periclase was then hauled away to join the desert iron oxide (that which was not split off and sold to the oil paint manufacturer), and these were then filtered and mixed with clay and sand and water, then pulverized together to form a stiff paste which was compressed and extruded through a die to slowly emerge as towers of glistening red brick in the Southern California afternoon sunlight. Aligned wires then sliced the brick towers into uniform blocks, and a vacuum pump sucked both the surface moisture and the beads of sweat that had dripped from the worker's forehead.

Once fired in ovens and cooled, the bricks were dehacked, automatically stacked, wrapped with steel bands, then padded with plastic corner protectors before being strapped to wooden palettes. Forklifted then, first by the factory, then by the railroad, then by the trucking company, then by the lumber wholesaler, who subsequently sold and re-loaded several of those palettes onto truck that hauled them to South Central Los Angeles, where they were unstrapped and tossed into disorder in the rusted tub of a wheelbarrow that rolled dozens of bricks at a time to the side of a mason on his knees at a corner gas station being newly remodeled. That 50 year-old immigrant from Italy, who had learned the trade from his father who had migrated here from Colorado when he was an infant, meticulously measured and laid and tapped and stacked hundreds of those bricks the same shape and color into neat rows of order once again—the top plane of that wall extending perfectly parallel to the line of the horizon.

It takes one ton of force to reduce the diameter of the human skull one centimeter. When Mrs. Denny's baby was born, like every baby in the ward, his skull was made up of 44 separate pieces. She would watch his pulse push the fine soft skin of his fontanel soft spot, that throb moving something deep inside her too as she sang him to sleep, as she prayed for his safety, and she would count the beats, with each pause a prayer sometimes, imagining the push of blood and the red of the tiny heart that once floated beneath her own. It would take thirty months for his anterior fontanel to close, just as it would for the 12 others born in the same ward that morning. And all who shared his birthday would, along with him, see the full ossification process begin twenty years later. And all would finish fusing uninterrupted decades later. All but Reginald Denny's.

At 6:46 p.m. on April 29, 1992, just minutes after a group of rioters threw rocks and forced him to stop his red dump truck carrying 27 tons of sand across the middle of the intersection of Normandy and Florence, after someone pulled him from the cab of that Transit Mixed Concrete Company truck, after someone stood on his neck and others kicked him in the abdomen, after someone hurled a 5-pound portable oxygenator at his head, after someone struck him with a claw hammer, just as Reginald Denny was trying to stand back up, a single red brick made from high desert iron oxide, lime, magnesia, clay, and sand was lifted high amidst the chaos and rage and thrown full-force from close range, shattering his cranium into more than 44 shards and fracturing his skull in 91 places, knocking him unconscious. After the brick thrower pointed and laughed and did a dance of victory in the street, after another spat on him, after others threw bottles at him, after his pockets were looted, after he finally came to and struggled to his hands and knees and tried to stand, the man with the hammer launched a flying kick to his face.

Once Reginald Denny rose at last, as he dragged himself back into the cab and started slowly zig-zagging away, it was then that four Good Samaritans approached, four individuals who had seen the entire incident unfolding live on their TVs from the reporters with video cameras in helicopters hovering overhead, four strangers who rushed together to that one flashpoint to help him get free and get to the hospital, and once the doctors there inserted a piece of plastic to prevent his dislocated eye from falling into his sinus cavity—it was then that someone drilled a hole in Reginald Denny's cranium to relieve the pressure, the same way the glistening wet towers of bricks were drilled so they could emerge from the tremendous heat of baking still intact.

After he regains his consciousness and his speech, after he goes through physical rehabilitative therapy, after he receives more than 27,000 get well cards (and places them in storage, refusing to throw a single one away as long as he remains alive)—although his speech and vision and natural gait are impaired, although he suffers permanent nerve damage and constant ringing in his ears, although his injured hippocampus means he always needs to carry a notebook and tape recorder to help his memory that comes and goes but mostly goes, although he is left with an indentation the size of a softball on the right side of his head—once in the courtroom at the trial of those men who are responsible for these maladies and for nearly killing him, after the jury of five whites, three blacks, three Latinos, and one Asian delivers the verdict, it is then that Reginald Denny slowly rises to his feet in front of his attackers, but this time instead of trying to flee he walks directly to those defendants' families, and Reginald Denny opens his arms and embraces the mothers of his assaulters one at a time, as an act of healing and consolation, causing one of the mothers, whose son had just been convicted of the felony of aggravated mayhem and sentenced to a maximum of ten years in prison, to say: "For those of you who don't understand, that's what you call real love."

When asked by the defense attorney during the trial if he was improving, Reginald Denny had said: "I'm doing okay. I'm getting better, yes, every day, hopefully, sir."

When asked 10 years later if he is angry, Reginald Denny says he isn't angry at the people who had rioted, because he knows he isn't their enemy, and that they aren't his, that they had felt abandoned by the police and the justice system, that their anger was fueled by the state of a city that the politicians had given up on, that it takes a lot of crap to happen before it stops happening but that sometimes neighborhoods get jacked up to the point that people will eventually just say enough is enough, they aren't going to give up or give in, and doesn't that say something about the character of the people that live here, that no matter how bad it gets, they aren't giving up? Reginald Denny says he knows the people didn't attack him because they hated him, they did it out of helplessness and disrespect for being disrespected.

Reginald Denny says that for all the media coverage focused on race, people forget that it was black people who saved his life, that while some were there trying to kill him or do him in, others were trying to save him. He says when people sent him the 27,000 letters to wish him well, an act of so much kindness he couldn't believe it, that those people were not concerned with race either. That they didn't care about color and he didn't care about color. That when he got blood in the hospital, no one checked to see what color the blood was, that it was probably red.

1850

SEAN HEARS the man's horse clomping up from the foothills ten minutes before he sees him, so Sean hides his wife and children in the house, and he sits on the porch. It's a trapper. It's always trappers or miners unless it's people from the Potwisha tribe, and it would be all right if the stranger were a part of the tribe, but Sean has hidden from white people all his married life.

Like Sean, the man is from Louisiana, but Baton Rouge, not New Orleans.

The man tells him that America made Zachary Taylor president.

"Really?"

"But he's already dead. A man named Millard Fillmore took over."

"Yeah," Sean says, and he wonders how long his wife can keep his baby boy silent.

"Also, they made California a state."

Sean cocks his head and thinks about that for a moment. "Why would they do that?"

The man laughs and shakes his head. "I don't know, but you're sitting in the United States of America."

Sean smiles because it's the smart move. Sean cheers because it's safe.

In an hour, the trapper moves on. In four hours, Sean and his wife have packed everything they will ever need to survive. In the afternoon, they are moving North and East, moving somewhere where there is no state or law. In a month, they are living gently with bears, wolves, and buffalo, creatures who would never convict them for miscegenation.

CONTINENTAL DRIFT

Tectonic plates separate. Seas turn to waterfalls to fill the chasms.

NATHANIEL

Nathaniel is on the 5 Freeway when he feels the pain in his chest and jaw, and he's been a surgeon long enough to know that he's having a heart attack, and that it's a big one, but what he would have thought would have made him panic only makes him think about his wife. It makes him think about that first date.

He thinks about driving down to Mexico and crossing the border, and letting Yessenia take him to her Tijuana. He thinks about laughing so hard, and how Mexico felt like freedom for him for all those months when they were dating and how it was like a new world for him and how he used to dream of Mexico and how he wished that he could just take whatever it was that the border had and just put it in himself so that Mexico would be with him always, that feeling, that difference.

He thinks about the end of that first date, how he'd crossed into America and glanced back and saw her waving at him shyly, and he'd stood there a moment, his fingers laced in the chain link fence in front of that no-man's land at the border. He had laughed for joy there for a moment, and then he had turned and gone home.

He feels like he's going to another border now to look across at her for a while, but maybe that's too romantic a notion for a moment like this, but he's always been a romantic and why not now too. He will ride his romance to the other side. He will wait there for her with his fingers laced through the fence, but he will not turn this time. He will not go home without her.

THE BONES

It was the child with eyes like sky who saw the gray one fall. The elder. He had folded first, she said. He bent over, put hands to knees, then tipped back, she said.

She had laughed. Then cried—but later, when she realized.

They had both been up before the sun. He to walk and think and gaze at the red star, the one that reminded him of the one he loved, that was no more of the spring. The one who had first turned gray with him. The one who had fallen, who had been covered right there on the trail behind them while he shook. The young girl had gotten up before the sun because she had heard a bird, she said.

The clan elder was covered there where he had fallen. There had once been many more in their group when they left the great hot basin for the last time, following the southern stars down the great valley to a new home by the marshes and rivers. Most of those who fell on the way were the gray ones. The fathers and mothers. The ones who had lived their lives side by side, but who in the end were left behind, without their mates, to sleep alone in unremembered places.

By the time the laughing then crying girl became a gray one, the clan had settled for good beside the cold flooding river. And it was there that she fell for the last time. It was there that her daughters wailed and tied bright strips around her ankles, the ankles of the elder one who had walked all the way from the birthplace of the gods. It was there she was covered for the last time, in line with others who had fallen in the seasons before, in the quiet place where all who fell were allowed to sleep undisturbed.

THE BALANCE OF THE TABLE

Juan rises in darkness, dresses in silence, prepares seven breakfasts with barely a sound so as not to awaken those loved ones still sleeping. Small hands, rough and marked but gentle as water. He draws a flower for each seat at the table (to be discovered later while they rub at their eyes, grinning). He knows that they will compare every petal—each face in the center, smiling. For now he considers each one with a nod, recovers those dreamers whose blankets have slipped off, kisses each forehead, whispers a prayer. Then he packs up three meals, a small pad and paper, and leaves for the bus that will take him to work. Two jobs. Back-to-back. He is building up more wealth for the ones who will pay him, he knows this, the ones with their daily bar charts showing profits, but he will bring back his own, too, for his own. For his family at home. And for those at the older table he left when he was young, he will do what he has always done and mail them what he's able.

SOUTH-WESTERN MIGRATION

S TONES STRUCK and chipped to fluted edges.
Narrow chute of flowing mountain carves the way to the great water.

ART IN THE WEST

Nancy comes west because train tickets that year are cheap and because the man said there was work out here for artists who are willing to put forth the effort. There are galleries he said, and Disney Studios opening up and looking for people who can paint backgrounds. There are movie studios all over.

Only, when the train jerks to a stop in the middle of the desert, she wakes up to see the vast tan world around her, a world that extends out into the forever. She can smell the earth here in a way she never could in the East. Everything makes a kind of sense, and she knows that just from looking out into the Mojave for three seconds. She understands her destiny in a way that she never has before, so she gathers her painting materials and luggage and steps off onto the platform, knowing that she'll never make it to Los Angeles, except maybe as a tourist.

The first day, she finds a cottage and takes her paints to the edge of town. The next day she finds a job that pays her enough to live. The third day, she settles into the ramble through the wildflowers and cacti, the painting and the walking, the silence and the dreaming, that she hopes will become her routine until the day of her death.

SIGNAL HILL

SHE SITS down with him next to the signal fire and stares out across the valley. Nothing to do until her brother comes up the hill to tell them what to signal. So she sits with her husband, back to back, him watching the ocean, her facing the mountains. She tells him the story of how she fell in love with him when she saw him gathering acorns, and they were still children. It's a story he's heard before. Still, he listens, laughing silently every once in a while, but she can feel his joy through his back.

She can feel when he stops listening too, when he goes rigid. They stand as a unit and stare out at the ocean where one of the giant ships she's heard of is gliding past. Something in her makes her smother the fire. Something knows that they don't want to signal these people. Something tells her to run, to leave this valley, to cross the mountains and flee into the desert to a small place where no one else lives, where she and her husband and whatever children they are blessed with can hide. They will drink morning dew if that is all there is. They will eat cacti and lizard tails. Something tells her that would be a better life than the one that is coming. She has heard about what these people do.

Except, the ship doesn't stop. It is going north, and her husband wraps his arms around her. They will stay here, she supposes, for now. They will wait until the very last moment to leave, but the moment one of the ships stops in her valley, they will cross into the void of the desert so she and hers can be forgotten forever and forever.

LAYERS

The cold flooding river swelled again and again. The river sang the songs of the mountain breath season after season. When the mud rode the banks up and over, it spilled out to become new ground, new blankets of fine earth carried from the high sacred places. Gray ones continued to fall. Those without creases too. The river mountain topsoil splashed over the quiet place again and again. Soon there were only the children of the children of the children falling, all descendants of the great clan from the north, in this village now called Yaanga, and all were buried on top of the older bones of the gray ones.

LOTS

The Viet Cong overrun Saigon in April, but it's not until June that Trung finds himself hidden with his cousin Xuan in the hold of his uncle's fishing boat. Xuan says that they should stay and fight. Better to die here fighting the bastards than drowning at sea. Besides, he says, they're going to be caught and sent to the reeducation camps if they are lucky.

Trung sits in the darkness with Xuan for days, asking him every once in a while to pray the rosary with him, and he thinks about the time he was in this boat when he was a little boy, the day they caught a catfish the size of a sun bear. It had been that month of great hunger, and the priest had them say a novena dedicated to St. Jude. On the ninth day of the novena, Xuan and his father struggled and struggled and pulled out a fish big enough to feed the world.

This time Xuan only laughs when Trung says they should pray. "We should have never left," he says. So Trung sits in the darkness of the hold for a week doing little more than dreaming about the fish and the war until his uncle comes down and tells the two boys that they can come outside.

After Trung is done blinking, he finds himself in the middle of a world gone to fog and water. "Where are we?" he asks his uncle.

He points directly behind them. "That's Viet Nam." His voice is confident.

"Where are we going?"

His uncle points straight ahead. "That's California."

Trung cocks his head. "I thought we were going to America."

All the men and women on board laugh and slap his back, and Trung laughs too when they explain the joke to him. They'd thought of going to Manila first, but it seems like unnecessary danger. Most refugees are in tiny crowded boats stacked with people trying to make it to Indonesia, but Trung is lucky. His uncle owns his own boat, and he knows the ocean.

Only in a week, his uncle has the sickness that makes him sweat. In two weeks, his uncle is dead.

They cast his body overboard and weep. The priest says his mass, and Trung thinks about the day when the old man caught his fish. He was the strongest man Trung had ever seen. Now, he will go back to his world of fish, and maybe that is the right place for him to rest. Maybe he will wash up on Viet Nam again. Maybe a catfish will swallow him whole and deliver him to Jesus. Trung likes to think of this. When he tells Xuan of his fantasy, Xuan looks like he might punch him in the face, so he only smiles.

In another month, the first mate is sure, absolutely sure, that they are less than a week from California.

The week after that, they cut down to half rations, and the priest suggests they say a novena. Of all the people on board, only Xuan refuses. Trung says he must put his faith in Jesus and in St. Jude, who is the patron saint of lost causes. "He will protect us."

Xuan chews on his lower lip. "It should have been you."

They take nine days to say their novena. When they are done, Trung stands on the deck of the boat staring out at the wide ocean wondering how it's going to happen. Maybe it will be a helicopter coming over the horizon. Maybe it will be Jesus walking across the ocean. Maybe a giant catfish will poke its head out of the water and lead them where they are going.

When nothing happens for two days, the priest says it is because Xuan has not prayed with them, and everyone stares anger at Xuan for cursing them. They cut down to one quarter rations, and the priest says maybe Xuan shouldn't get a ration at all. "This boat is for the faithful," he says. He paints a black cross on the deck and turns to Xuan. "This boat is for God."

In two days, they begin on a new novena, and Xuan stays away from them. He keeps his face dark. He is always angry these days, but so is nearly everyone else. As far as he can tell, only Trung remains hopeful. He knows that Jesus has a better life waiting for him in the new world.

On the eighth night of the novena, Trung dreams that the boat comes aground on California. He wakes up smiling, and he laughs at little nothings all day waiting for the prayer to start. After they finish, he goes to the stern of the boat and stares out across the waves. He wants to be the first to shout to everyone about the land. He stays there for two days until the priest comes to him and tells him that there is going to be a meeting.

At the meeting, the priest says his words and weeps his prayers. Then they place thirty pieces of paper in a bucket, one for every person on the boat except for the priest. Even before they start, Trung knows that it will be Xuan who gets the piece of paper with the pencil mark on it.

Xuan must know it too because when the crew member walks to him with the hammer, he does not struggle, beg, or run. He merely kneels down to make it easier for the man. He hangs his head as if in prayer.

Later, after everyone has eaten, the priest tells them that a new novena will start tomorrow, and no one disagrees. What else is there to do? Trung thinks about Xuan and his father and that day they caught the fish, and he thinks about how good it tasted, how meaty. He thinks about California and Viet Nam. He thinks about Jesus walking across the waves.

When he dreams that night, he sees Xuan happy now on the California shore beyond the world of pain and cares. When he wakes up in the morning, he decides that this time he will be the one not to pray. He will call the priest's eye to him, and he will receive the blessing given first to his uncle and then to his cousin, Xuan.

THE THREE STRIKES RULE

On December 8th, Danielle's brother calls her and tells her that his son is off to war in Japan or Germany, he doesn't know which, but he hopes it's Japan because they deserve it more. He says that he's going to have to take care of Greg's wife Maria and their boy, and Danielle immediately offers to move in with him.

"You don't have to."

She thinks about her answer and says, "Since Sue's passed, you'll need me." What she really wants to say is that she doesn't want to leave Maria alone in a house with a man like him. She wants to tell him that little Oscar needs protection too, and she wishes that she could just take mother and son into her home and shut out her brother forever, but she can't think of a way to put that into words, so she packs three bags instead and goes.

It starts out almost friendly. In the first weeks, when people come out, he refers to Maria as his Mexican daughter and then as his dirty little Mexican daughter in the weeks after that, but he says it with a smile. After that, he drops the "daughter" and then the smile. By the summer, her brother is drinking again, and the California desert heat keeps them inside near the swamp cooler, everything inside a little moist and cool, the world that Danielle watches outside baking and tan.

It surprises Danielle that it takes so long for it to happen. Her brother doesn't get drunk enough to hit Maria until late August, and when he does, and when Maria locks herself in her bedroom, and when Oscar starts wailing so loud that her brother curses him, Danielle takes the bottle of bourbon she's had hidden and waiting for this moment, and she gives it to her brother who drinks himself into what she knows will be a long and dreamless sleep. That's when she knocks softly on Maria's door and takes her and her grandnephew to her house in town.

By September, her brother has moved from threats to apologies and tears, and by mid-October, the gifts begin to show up at her doorstep, first a whistle for Oscar, the boy he calls his brown little berry. Then some cash in an envelope with a note explaining that it's his duty, and she doesn't have to talk to him, but he hopes she will let him see the boy. Then a winter jacket because the cold is coming and books in Spanish and English and then a bicycle for Oscar who is not yet two years old.

In November, he knocks on the door and demands that Danielle let him see his little half-breed, and she says that he can't, and he says he'll kill her, and she can smell the alcohol on his breath so she excuses herself and gets the bottle of bourbon that she's been saving for today and presents it to him like a consolation. Four hours later, she gets a call from the police station, an officer who wants to know if she'd like to bail him out.

"Let him rot," she says. "Tell him that was his last chance."

She, Maria, and Oscar have a happy Christmas and a peaceful New Year, and they don't hear from her brother until late January when he calls, and Danielle picks up the telephone.

"You can't force me out of their lives," he says.

"I told the policeman that was your last chance."

His silence through the phone is as loud as her father's silences were all those years ago. She can see his face going red. She knows that he's rubbing that white scar on his finger. "You're barely even family."

"I'm her family in a way you'll never be. I need to know that you're going to leave Oscar and Maria alone. I'm taking care of them now."

"If I have to come over there . . ." He leaves these last words hang in the wire between them.

She takes a breath.

"I swear to God, if I have to come down there. . ."

"Tell you what," she says. "Why don't we talk about this? I'll come down to see you."

Danielle finds the bottle of bourbon that she's been saving specifically for today, and then she goes downtown and buys a second bottle. When she gets out into the desert to her brother's house, she hands him one of the bottles. "Drinking was the only thing Dad ever taught us that was useful," she says.

They laugh. The old joke.

It cuts the tension somehow, and her brother pulls out two water glasses, and they drink and laugh and talk about the old days. When they're most of the way through the bottle, she says that she'd better go home, and he nods and gets up to go to bed as she knew he would. She listens to him climb into bed, and she waits patiently for him to begin to snore.

When he's deep asleep, she opens the other bottle and pours out most of it on his bed around him. She lights a cigarette, and drops it on the bed near his hand. She doesn't leave until the bed is in flames, and she doesn't hurry. She's too drunk to drive, so it's important not to hurry tonight. She needs to be there for her Maria. She needs to be safe to care for her little Oscar.

THE SAVIOR

Early in 1930, Jesus learns to keep his name to himself. Some Anglo men he's getting a ride from can't believe that he's named for the savior. Laughing, they pull him out of the car and beat him for blasphemy. Later that year, Jesus realizes that when he cuts his hair short and wears a baseball cap, white people think he's one of them as long as he doesn't speak. From that moment, he starts to work on his accent, so he can move in and out of their world. He even puts an Okie twang on some of his words so the people at the soup kitchens give him whatever they have. When someone asks his name, he tells them he's Jerry Johnson, but he does what he can to keep to himself.

It's not until 1932 that Jesus tries to sleep in the same Hooverville as the Anglos. It's like a game really, Jesus setting up his own little shanty and sleeping among all those people who have a leg up. In the mornings, he starts moving in the cold and waits with the other men on the roadside for work, blowing warm air into his hands and pacing back and forth to heat himself up just like the rest of them. In the evenings, he nods at their women and thinks of his wife and boys at home.

On a morning in January, Jesus wakes up before dawn to the sound of men talking outside his shack about a lead on a job they have up North, and he's out and following the men to the road. He hopes that they're going to be put in the back of a truck and driven to this mysterious place in the north. Then he can keep the brim of his cap over his eyes and stand with them, and he will be one of them, but these men have their own truck, and when they all pile in, there is no room in the cab or the bed. They all know each other and watch him darkly.

The camp feels empty when he comes back even though most

of the men are still here, and he walks back to his place with his hands in his pockets until he hears someone calling. "Jerry, Jerry." It's a woman's voice. When he looks around, a woman is standing near a campfire waving at him. The sky has just begun to blue, and the orange of the firelight casts her in a warm light where everything else in this world is cold.

When he comes over, she says, "Do you know me?"

Jesus cocks his head at her. "I don't think so," he says. He wouldn't have looked at her before, but he sees her now, beautiful in her way. She's not a classic, but there's strength in her face that makes him think of other women he has loved.

"No," she says. "I've watched you. You know my son though. Don't you? Donny?"

"Donny? The little boy?"

As he comes closer, the smell of frying meat fills his nose. He's not sure what it is exactly, but she seems to have a lot of it going on a skillet in the fire. "Donny's not a little boy any longer. He just looks like it."

"How old is he?"

"Twelve, nearly thirteen, but he's small and looks younger than he is."

Jesus would have guessed the boy was twelve, but he plays along, sitting across from her. Maybe this Anglo woman will help him to get work. Maybe she will share her food.

As if she is reading his mind, she begins to scoop whatever is in the skillet onto a dish. "He's nearly thirteen, but he can't get any work because he's small." She starts to hand it to him but pulls back. "His father left us last year."

"I'm sorry." He says this to the plate of food.

"When he was with us, he could get work picking cotton or fruit, and they'd hire Donny on with him because he was part of the family. Donny gets some jobs now, but not like he did back when his father was with us. Some of those farmers want a family working for them."

Jesus knows what she's hinting at, but he thinks about his own wife and boys he sees once a year when he hitches his way back home. He thinks about the men who beat him that day as they joked about the blasphemy of his name.

"You're alone," she says.

"Yes, I am."

"So are Donny and me."

"Yes." He's supposed to say more, he knows, but he doesn't know how to answer. She hands him the plate, and he eats a forkful, understanding that this bribe represents the last bit of food she has, and that she has given more to him than she's saved for herself and her son combined.

"Do you want a family?"

Jesus looks down at his food and thinks about his wife and the time he has been here. He thinks about this northern world, and he scrapes most of the food back into the skillet. "Yes," he says. "I'd like that very much. Eat. Call Donny out here. Give him some food."

She's right. A family is a good thing. At least, that is, some farmers do seem to prefer nice white families to lone Mexican men roaming around asking for work, so he will be like her husband. Like her real husband, he will work with her and for her, and he will save his money. He will teach her son how to work and be a man. Finally, like her husband, one day not too long from now, when he has earned money, he will disappear from her life. He will slip back down to Mexico where his wife waits for him far from this place where the name Jesus is so strange to people.

PART TWO
SYMBOLS OF HUMAN FAILURE

"We often say how impressive power is. But I do not find it impressive at all. The guns and the bombs, the rockets and the warships, are all symbols of human failure."

— Lyndon B. Johnson

THE GOLDEN GATE BRIDGE

STELLA WAKES up in the passenger seat on the Golden Gate Bridge just in time to look into the eyes of the man who's standing on the wrong side of the railing and about to jump. Before she has a moment for horror, she recognizes him, one of her men from when she was a nurse. She can't place exactly who he is, but she's sure he was an officer who was shot in Germany and came through her ward, maybe from Arden. She remembers the look on his face when he found out that he'd lost something, a leg, his company, or his wife, something like that. She remembers the feeling of his arms as she held him and wept with him. She remembers the smell of rubbing alcohol, and his breath on her neck. Before she has a chance to be terrified, she smiles and thinks about the way he kissed her on the cheek when she told him the lie she told everyone, that it was going to be all right, that everything was going to be just fine. His kiss wasn't filled with desperate need. It was tender, brotherly, and in her half-dream state, she touches the place where his lips brushed her face. Even five years later, she can feel the scrub of his stubble and the warmth of his lips.

IN THE TULE FOG

Hai Nguyen sees the shaggy dog from his living room window. It's curled up on top of something under a tree on the shoulder of Highway 99. It's looking around, as if guarding something. Hai's mother has told him that he cannot leave the apartment on his own until America has won the war in Vietnam, so he has to wait for her to go into her bedroom for a moment. When she does, he snatches a banana and slips out the front door, closing it gently, without a click.

Taking the stairs two at a time, Hai names the dog Brontosaurus Rex. When there is a break in traffic, he runs across the street and laces his fingers through the chain link fence and calls, "Rex-O." He breaks off a piece of the banana and holds it through the fence for the dog who watches him but does not move. "Rex," he calls again.

When Brontosaurus Rex barks, whatever he's lying on moves. He has been guarding a man in his sleep, who stirs now. He's as shaggy as the dog and wrapped in a big green jacket. When the man sees Hai, he makes a kind of stomach grunt and sits up, pushes backward against a tree trunk. "Peace," the man yells, but it's a kind of warning.

Hai can feel the tears coming, but he pushes them down the way his mother showed him. He drops the banana piece, and he knows that he should run, but he can't make himself.

The man eyes him with a frown. "No," he says. "You're all right, aren't you?"

Hai nods. It's the most he can get out.

"You're not here for me are you?" He wipes his eyes and looks around him as if he is trying to figure out this strange world of fog and traffic noise.

"I like your dog."

The man wraps his arms around the dog as though Hai is here to steal it, and Hai wonders if the dog's fur is soft or rough.

"How far is it?"

"What?"

"Saigon," the man says. It's a name that Hai has heard, but he doesn't recognize it exactly. Sometimes, the adults say it, he thinks. The man points north. "Saigon," he says. "How far?"

Hai shrugs. "Not Saigon. Sacramento."

"Sacramento," the man says, and he hugs the dog to himself.

Hai is across the street again, but he cannot pull himself away completely. The man is back there talking to his dog, saying something that Hai cannot hear, but he can hear the man's tone. His voice sounds like his mother's when she talks about his sister, his brother, his grandmother, his aunt, his father.

ALL OF THOSE BOYS ARE DEAD NOW

It's March when Everett's wife comes down to the shop to tell him that his baby brother has left for Europe. Jon said he was going to enlist, but Everett figured he meant to finish high school at least. Everett hoped that in the time it took Jon to graduate and cross the entire continent to sign up for service, the war would be over. He's never spoken that thought to anyone, knows how its premise is rooted in cowardice, but he's always known that he has no backbone when it comes to his brother or his wife or his son.

Jon must have known of his fear. That's why he lit out without telling him. Now that the weather's good and everyone's coming into Everett's little store, they both know there's nothing he can do to stop his little brother. What he can do is sell clothing, make himself smile, and think about his brother standing knee deep in trench water waiting for the Huns to charge over the edge. He's read about Europe. Everyone knows what it's like.

In June, Everett gets a formal note from the government saying Jon died in a training accident, but in July another one comes saying that the first note was a mistake. Someone else named Jon Mitchell died, not Everett's brother. That August, Everett decides to build his sixteen-year-old brother a house, next to his, overlooking the Eel River.

On a late August Sunday afternoon, Everett's clearing the moss off a boulder when he comes across the ancient pictures. They're dim, but he can see them sketched in red and yellow dyes or paint. They're stick figures, kind of, but there are big circle things too, elaborate designs that look like someone's religion from way back.

When Mary comes out of the house to check up on him, Everett's sitting cross-legged in the dirt in front of the boulder staring at it. She sits down next to him and puts her hands on his leg. "That's what I think it is, isn't it?"

"I'm almost sure of it." Back when they were going to school, they'd had a teacher who taught them about these kinds of pictures.

"If they see it . . ." Mary doesn't have to finish the sentence. She doesn't have to say who "they" are.

"So we won't let anyone see."

Everett stands and picks up the sledgehammer he's been busting stones with all week. He hefts it and stares at the pictures, but something stops him. Maybe he's a coward. That's it, he decides. He just can't bring himself to destroy something with that kind of historical power.

Mary watches him. He knows she supports him, but when he puts his hammer down, she smiles at him and nods her righteousness. He throws a tarp over the boulder instead, and he's glad about that. Twenty minutes later a Sunday school class full of ten-year-olds come chattering down the road on their way to a picnic. They flow onto his property like the ocean, asking him about Jon and the house for two minutes of chaos before they flow out again.

"We need something better than a tarp," Everett says.

"All we need is for the moss to grow back."

It's true, but they need something until then.

In September, Everett takes the tarp back off to see if there's been any growth, but of course, the tarp has kept anything from growing at all. It's the first time he's seen the paintings since that day, and they look no different. In that time, he has brought three hired men onto his property, and Mary's folks have come over for dinner. When people are around, he worries about them relentlessly. When he is away, he thinks about them in the same way he used to think about Jon.

He works on the house through October and November when the weather is good. He buys an extra pallet of bricks, which he stacks in front of his boulder, like it's there only waiting to be used for some building project.

He's ready to put the finishing touches on the house in December. He'll paint if he has a dry day, but then he gets another formal note from the government saying that Jon is dead. This time he's supposed to have been shot during a charge.

And so Everett waits for the follow-up note saying that someone made a mistake again. He smiles and shakes his head at the way the government can foul these things up, and when Mary cries into her hands, he holds her and tells her it's probably all just a mistake. Everything will be right in a month or two.

By February, Everett finally has the feeling that no note is coming, and on the first of March he tells Mary that they should write to the university and tell someone about the paintings. Someone is going to want to study them.

"What about Jon's house?" she asks.

But Everett shrugs. He's a coward when it comes to these kinds of things. He doesn't think he has it in him to fight or to hide.

§

The day Everett's son comes home from Japan, Everett asks him what he wants to do now that he's back.

"I really just want to walk down by the Eel River," he says.

Everett meant more like did he want to get married or start a business or something like that, but taking a walk along the Eel sounds just about right for the first day home. When Everett starts to put on his shoes, Sam smiles at him. "I kind of wanted to go down there and think about things by myself."

Everett tries to understand, does understand in his way. It makes sense, he thinks. There's no knowing what the young man might have seen or done, if he's been a coward or hero. Everett suspects that his son's been a hero, but maybe that's hard, too.

By the time Sam comes back four hours later, Everett's about ready to go out looking for him.

The next morning when Everett comes down for breakfast, Sam's gone out already, and he stays out until nearly one in the afternoon.

"Maybe he's gotten a job," Mary says.

But when Sam comes home, and Everett asks him where he's gone, Sam says, "I was just walking and thinking."

"Thinking about what?"

Sam narrows his eyes, leans against the door frame, and folds his arms. "I don't know." He's stumped by the question. Really stumped. Disturbed maybe, too, but he sits down and starts to eat the leftover lunch Mary gives to him.

"You want to talk about anything?" Everett asks.

"No." Sam coughs into his plate.

Everett looks into his eyes, wonders what's back there, wonders what kind of guilt he feels, terror, anything. He wishes there was something he could do, some kind of action that he could take to make things even a little better. He thinks about his brother who died in a war. He thinks about his neighbor, Frank's sons, how one day when they were all young, he took all those boys rafting, all five of them and Sam and Mary and Frank, too. He thinks about how it was a foggy day, but they said the heck with it and rafted straight into the fog, and they had two rafts and there were times when he couldn't see the other one, but he knew they were there because the laughter of those kids came skipping across the water, and how they all got silent at that moment when they got close to shore and saw a bear standing by himself. They saw bears all the time, but they knew this one was special.

All of those boys are dead now except for Sam, and Everett wishes that he could do something for any of them, wishes he knew what is missing right now except the kids and that laughter.

Everett lies in bed awake that night. When dawn begins to blue the room, he gets dressed and goes downstairs to wait. Five minutes later Sam comes out and walks to the door. Everett says, "Could I join you today?"

They go out into the cold Northern Californian morning, one that reminds Everett of that day twenty years ago on the rafts. They plunge their hands in their pockets and walk down toward the river.

"So," Everett says. "Where are you thinking about doing?"

Everett meant should they go right or left on the river, but Sam says, "I don't know. They offered me the job as bank manager again. The owners says there's a raise in it for me since I was an officer. Maybe I'll do that."

"I didn't know that. Are you going to take it?"

Everett shrugs. "I don't know. It seems pointless."

The hopelessness of his son's tone knots Everett's stomach. "It's good pay. You could settle down."

"Maybe," Sam says. "I'm not sure I want to settle. Maybe I want to get that Ph.D."

"Philosophy?"

Sam shrugs. "Maybe. Maybe business. I was thinking about Eastern religions, too." They're walking on the bank, and Sam looks up into the sky.

"What are you looking for?"

Everett means is he looking up into the sky for an eagle or did he hear an airplane or something like that, but Sam says, "I'm looking for something bigger. I don't know if that makes sense."

"I think it does," Everett says. "You want something more than bank management."

"Yeah, I want to find something good in my life."

"Do you remember the day on the rafts when we saw that bear?" Everett asks.

"That was a good day. When I was in Japan, we saw a moon bear. This is after the war was over. I was with four other guys in the mountains, and it was in a tree. I told my buddy about that day we saw the bear in the fog and what it meant to me. Then he shot the bear."

"Why'd he do that?"

Sam shrugs. "I don't know. He'd been to Nagasaki and watched a lot of people die. Maybe it had to do with that. Maybe he was just a hunter."

There's a meaning down at the bottom of Sam's story, but Everett doesn't know how to get at it. It explains all the losses the world has felt in the last ten years. It means something to Sam, but there's no way in for Everett. What does it matter anyway? Everett will walk with his son. He'll listen to him talk. He'll help him if he can. Maybe tomorrow he'll suggest rafting, and maybe Sam will say yes. It won't be the same as it was before the war, but maybe that's all right, too.

§

Two mornings after his grandson's high school graduation, Everett walks next door to his son's house before dawn, slips in, and wakes Carl. Except for his shoes, he's already dressed and packed, and the two of them are out the door before Everett's son, wife, or daughter-in-law are awake or have a chance to argue with them.

They get into Everett's truck and head north toward Canada,

but they get only as far as Eureka just as the sun is beginning to rise, and Carl asks him to turn around.

Everett pulls over on the road in front of a breakfast place. "You don't want to go to Canada?"

"What would I do up there?"

"You don't have to do anything. I have four thousand dollars for you. Just live on that for a while until you figure things out."

"I don't know, Grandpa."

"It's your choice," Everett says. He looks at him directly, like he's a man, which he soon will be. "But if you stay, they're going to send you to Viet Nam."

"Yeah." Everett gives it another fifteen minutes, but he knows it's hopeless, and he turns around.

They're back home and downstairs making breakfast at Everett's house before anyone gets up.

The next week, Everett is awakened in the middle of the night by Carl at his bedside. Mary's breathing next to him is unbroken as he gets out of bed and grabs some clothes. They make it all the way to Grants Pass, Oregon this time before they turn around.

"I want you to know what a bad idea it is for you to stay here," Everett tells him when they stop for lunch in Crescent City. "My brother died in the First World War."

Carl shrugs with affected courage. "Dad made it through World War II."

Everett tries to make himself look wise by staring wistfully out the diner's window. "Your father came back changed."

"Dad would never forgive me for leaving."

"Your father can fuck things," Everett says. He blushes. It's the first time he's ever cursed, and he knows he got it wrong. He looks around to see if maybe the waitress heard him, but if she did, she doesn't care.

Anyway, it makes Carl smile, and he nods.

"I'll take you up to Vancouver, and you can live on that $4000 for a long time. Give me your address when you get settled, and I'll send you more money."

Carl stares into his eggs.

He doesn't say anything, so Everett says, "Your father will forgive you. Fathers always do." But that's not true. If Carl dies in some war that even Walter Cronkite says is wrong, just to please his father, Everett knows that he'll never forgive his son.

Everett's read about that war, knows what's going on there. He knows about napalm and Agent Orange. Somehow in his old age, he's come to hate war, or maybe he's just a coward. He doesn't know. He doesn't remember being a coward like this when he was younger, but maybe he was.

Nothing Everett says makes any difference to Carl, and they drive back home before dinner time. When Mary asks him where they were, Everett says, "Fishing. I told you last night we were going fishing. Don't you ever listen?"

Everett wakes up at 3:30 every morning for the next ten days. When he gets up, he goes outside in that space between his house and his son's house, next to the mossy boulder that's right under Carl's window. He waits for the light that never turns on, and he watches the stars and listens for bears. Each morning, he imagines that moment when they'll cross the border, and Carl will be safe. He thinks about how he'll visit his grandson every once in a while. He wonders how long it will take for his own son to begin to hate him.

On the tenth night, Everett hears a door open. He hears the crunch of boots on gravel. "Carl," he says.

"No." It's his son's voice. He looms up to Everett in the darkness.

"You're up early this morning." He can't see Sam's face, doesn't know how angry he is or if he's angry at all, but knowing Sam, he probably is.

"He got the letter yesterday," Sam says. "The one from the government."

"The draft?"

"The draft." He can hear Sam take a deep breath. "Take this." It's a moment before Everett understands what it is, but he figures out it's an envelope stuffed as full as it can get. "That's two thousand dollars. When you take him this time, make sure not to stop until you're across the border."

AS THE CITY BURNS

A WEEK after Jose is out of basic training, the Rodney King trial ends, and he finds himself holding a rifle in Los Angeles, two miles away from the house where he grew up. His job as he understands it is to stand here with Fleck and watch poor people burn down their businesses. For now, they can kill themselves and each other, but he and Fleck have their rifles to make sure no poor person passes the invisible line he stands on that separates the people who have lawns and the people who do not.

It's like that for seven straight hours before anyone actually approaches Jose's corner from behind, a man from the area of town where people live in ranch houses and pay his aunts to scrub the undersides of their toilet rims, slams the door of his black car.

"You can't be here," Fleck says, and Jose watches closely. He lifts his rifle a little, just enough to let the man know.

The man stops, loosens his tie, laughs, and raises his hands as if they're all old frat-boy buddies. "Hey. I'm a friend. I'm on your side."

"You can't be here," Jose says. "Turn around."

"I just need a minute of your time." He points at the second story of a building just on the other side of the barrier. "I work there. I need something out of my office."

"Out of that building?" Fleck asks.

Jose can hear the reasonableness in Fleck's voice, hears him already giving in to the threat suggested by his second chin, so Jose speaks first, "You need to disperse right now."

"Garcia," Fleck says as though Jose is overreacting, and maybe he is, but today overreaction seems to be the official policy.

"You want to let him through?"

Fleck cocks his head as if to ask, "What would it hurt?"

"We've been keeping people from crossing this street all day. What makes him special?"

"Garcia, is it?" The man pulls his wallet from his pocket. I've been sitting on my hands for days now. I have a client who just won't wait any longer." He pulls what looks like ten or twenty bills out of his wallet. "I don't expect you to do this just because you're a nice guy, and I can see how hard you're working."

Jose stares through the bills and out the other side until he sees his mother and grandfather living inside all of that smoke, sees them spending that money. Only, in this moment, Jose hates the man's lip-licking face, so he aims the sight at the middle of his chest. "Sir, I am authorized to shoot anyone who tries to force his way across this line."

Perhaps, this is not technically a lie.

When the man gets into his Mercedes, Fleck says, "Dude."

The way he says it, it becomes an accusation.

"This is the line," Jose says. "No one goes past it."

No one does, not for the moment Jose is here watching his hometown burn itself in a sulfur that turns black, that rises, that blows itself out over the Pacific Ocean, that disappears into the sky above those endless waters.

POST-WAR

THE CHILD runs with a blue pail of sea water, up the banking sand. His wobbly legs bunch together as he falls forward, the water creating a momentary curve of silver in the morning sky. He is too far away for her to save him.

Her smile fades as she springs to her feet and runs to sweep him up into her arms.

As his sobbing fades, she notices the moon, pale, above his head.

The castles they built, she thinks, will be gone by the next full moon. She kisses the top of his head. His hair is salty and warm. She thinks of his father's hair. She feels the sand on her lips and closes her eyes, thinks of the individual grains, how they bind together. She remembers how she craved salty things when he was forming in her belly. How that thirst never went away.

THE BOMBING OF GOLETA

Lawrence lifts himself out of the hospital bed he's had installed in his living room when he hears the first explosion down the beach. He knows it's the Japanese finally bombing the West Coast. He's been waiting for the invasion since Pearl Harbor, but he isn't afraid. He takes his pistol, flashlight, and cane and walks out the back door onto the beach.

He decides that this will be his last night, but what a way to go. The percussive thud of the bombs that must be landing down in Goleta is a full-body experience. He feels it even in his knees, and the explosions light the hills, each one shining yellow on to the scrub. Soon, he prays, the Japanese forces will rise out of the ocean, mounting the shore from their crafts, and he will be here to meet them.

This is the way for an old cavalry man to go. Pistol in hand screaming at the bastards. It's so much better than what he's been dreading, relatives lounging next to him for long months of unmanning, all of them hoping it would come sooner, him most of all.

Bombs thud the ground a quarter mile down the beach, and he shouts. The town is in a blackout, but on the beach, he takes out his flashlight and points it to the ocean. Let the bastards start here. Let him be their landing beacon. He drops his cane and levels his pistol, shooting rounds into the darkness that will soon swell with death.

Let it come tonight, now.

ZOOT SUIT RIOTS

MAGDALENA NEVER goes inside the movie house because she does not speak enough English to dream these fantasies, but she loves to stop and look at the posters. Today, she stares into the joyous face of Bernadette, dressed plainly, but caught in a vision of heaven.

When the soldiers who will be fighting Japanese soon begin to pull the young men out of the front door of the theater, she is lost in her dreams of the saint, and she stands there dumbly for a moment until she is caught inside their flood. In the time it takes to snap back into this world, they have begun to beat brown people, and she stands looking helplessly for a place to run.

She would scream, but she has her vision of Bernadette, this woman who brought water and peace to her people, who brought the virgin, and she knows that it is her place to confront their anger with the love of a saint. Love fills her even as the Anglo men in uniforms begin to tear at her clothes, as they scream words she will never know, as she feels the first thud on the temple of her body.

WE'LL BE THINKING OF YOU

R IGHT BEFORE the noon bell, the teacher tells the class there will be a special event at the end of the day. Cheers erupt. When the teacher doesn't smile along with everyone and quickly changes the subject, Ken knows it's about him. At the lunch bell, he walks straight to the bathroom, and 10 minutes later his friends on the playground notice he's standing off by himself out on the kickball diamond. They go running over to him.

"Ken!" Hugh shouts as they approach. "What do you think it is? I say Hedy Lamarr is coming. Claire says a person's not a special event."

When they get nearer, they can see Ken is crying. He turns away, and everyone grows quiet and stops before they get to him. Except for Hugh, who walks up and lays his arm across his friend's shoulder. He puts his mouth close to his ear and whispers something. Ken shakes his head. Hugh looks to the group and sweeps his other arm, signaling them to leave.

All afternoon his classmates are looking over at Ken, but he keeps his head down on the desk, and they know something is really wrong because Mrs. Phinney doesn't even make him sit up straight.

At 2:00 Principal MacGrueter walks in and calls for Ken to please follow her. Several girls gasp as Ken stands up and walks out, tears streaming down his face. Veronica starts crying even though she doesn't know why.

Elizabeth raises her hand and speaks before being called on. "Mrs. Phinney, why is Ken in trouble?"

Mrs. Phinney walks to the front of her desk and leans against it, her arms folded, head down. She is silent a moment, then she looks up. Her face is pale.

"Ken will no longer be attending Washington Irving Junior High," she says. Moans and gasps from the class, and Veronica starts crying harder. Before Mrs. Phinney can compose herself enough to explain, most of the girls are crying too.

"But, what did he do wrong?" Hugh asks.

"Nothing. He did nothing wrong. Ken is a good boy. He—She puts the back of her hand to her mouth.

"Is he sick?" Hugh asks.

Mrs. Phinney shakes her head. "No. No, he's not sick."

She looks around at the faces of her students. "I'm sorry, class. Ken and his family are moving to Arcadia. There's a camp there, at the race track, where all of the Japanese families will be living for a while."

"But why?" Ambrose asks.

"Because of the war."

"But—"

"I know."

§

That afternoon a man in a black suit and a man in a military uniform walk into the school's office just as Mrs. Phinney is leading the class out to the kickball diamond at the far end of the field. Hugh and Ken have their arms draped across each other's shoulders as they walk. Most of the girls are crying. Some of the boys, too.

Mrs. Phinney tells the class to circle around, and she stands at home plate and calls Ken over. She holds out a giant card made of thick construction paper, "We'll Be Thinking of You" is printed in large letters across the front.

"The class made this today for you to take with you, and remember us by. We all signed it."

Ken takes it and everyone claps. Then everything grows quiet. No one knows what to say. Hugh looks away just as a breeze hits, blowing his hair slightly, and he sees the man in the suit and the man in the military uniform standing by the tetherball pole on the far side of the blacktop. They are staring at the children. Hugh gets angry.

"This isn't right," Hugh says.

"Well, I know this is hard," Mrs. Phinney answers, "but our president tells us that the relocation of Japanese families are to ensure everyone's safety during—"

"But Ken and his family are Americans," Hugh interrupts. "Tell them, Ken."

Mrs. Phinney allows his speaking out of turn, considering. Besides, she was thinking the same thing.

"My parents are *Nisei*, which means second generation."

Mrs. Phinney looks around to the class, gathered in a circle. "'Second generation' meaning the second generation in the U.S. They were born citizens."

"And Ken's a citizen, too," Hugh says. "His whole family is. Why are they locking up Americans?"

"My grandparents are Issei. Not citizens," Ken says. Ken remembers the stories his grandfather told him, of fleeing Japan to become a strawberry farmer, starting his own business, and how his grandmother was a picture bride who came later.

"But they are friends. We're locking up good people."

Just then cheers erupt from across the schoolyard as all of the classroom doors open and students come streaming out. Everyone on the field turns to look, the wind gusting now. The school day has ended early so they can join Ken's class and say goodbye. Hundreds of seventh and eighth graders start to run at them, shouting. The teachers are coming out too, each one carrying a large card made from colorful construction paper, each card signed by every student in the class.

Ken, who had stopped crying on the walk out to the field, feels the tears welling now, and he laughs slightly. He is shaking. He looks down to the card he is holding and sees all of the hand-drawn hearts and words from his classmates start to blur with his tears as the voices around him grow louder.

THE VIEW FROM PORCUPINE HILL

AT NOON, Imelda brings Eduardo his lunch where he's working on top of Signal Hill. Now everyone has started calling it Porcupine Hill because of how many oil derricks poke out of the top of it like quills. He's holding dynamite, getting ready to do the job she hates the most. Somehow, it's always Eduardo who is chosen to light the fuse and drop it down the well, and he has to do it cheerfully, has to hide the palsy that started last year and is getting worse every day, or they'll fire him. In the last couple months, people have started calling him Clumsy Eddie. They laugh and pat him on the back.

Imelda wants to go to him now, but John, Eduardo's boss, limps over to her. "Give him a couple of minutes." He's pretending too. She knows that he doesn't like her to see his limp, the fact of it. She see the way he acts differently when she's around, the way he smiles shyly, his ears reddening, but knows that he would never take another man's wife.

"Why does he always have to light the fuse?" she asks.

"He volunteers." John shrugs and smiles. "I think he likes the boom."

"He does," she says, even though she knows how much he hates it.

When the young men were around, they would beg for a chance to play with the explosives, to drop them down the well where they would go off and set up a geyser of water and oil. It makes pumping easier somehow. It was fun for them, she supposes, the danger and the power that shakes the ground. Only those kids are gone now, off to Europe to kill a man called the Kaiser.

Soon she thinks, Eduardo will get his notice to go to Europe, too. At forty-four, he's just on this side of young enough. When he does, she'll ask him to run with her.

Right now, he faces away from her and the rest of the men, but even from here, she can see that his hands are shaking. He stiffens his back the way he does when he's trying to maintain control as though flexing all of his muscles at once will keep a steadiness.

He tries to strike a match but drops it and the box and the stick of unlit dynamite.

John laughs and shakes his head at what he must think is just Eduardo's clumsiness, but Imelda takes a step forward, starts to walk to him.

"Wait," John says. "Give him a second."

When Imelda takes another stumbling step forward, he puts a hand on her shoulder, not grasping and hard like she would have expected from a man like him. He's firm but gentle. If a hand can be understanding, it's that.

"I need to tell him something," she says. She can see Eduardo using his left hand to steady his right. He takes a deep breath. He is saying words to himself.

"He'll just be a minute." There's something in John's voice that makes her turn to him. He is staring at her carefully, a good man, a smart man trying to understand what is happening. She could run to Eduardo if she wanted to. The leg John lost fighting in Mexico would mean he could only limp behind, but then he would know something is wrong. He would try to find a way to keep her man working, but soon enough, he would have to fire him for everyone's sake.

So Imelda smiles. "Yes," she says.

"I'm going to miss Eddie when he goes."

"When he goes?"

"He told me that he got his draft card last week."

"Oh," she says, trying not to look shocked. "Yes, well, I'll miss him more."

He has been lying to her then, but she understands that he just wants everything to be good. "Do you have family nearby?"

"No, everyone's back in Mexico."

"Well, if you need . . ." Somehow, he cannot finish the sentence when she turns to him and looks him in the eyes. She knows how the sentence ends, though. She knows that she cannot respond to it, and he does, too.

When they both turn back to Eduardo, he is striking the match again, over and over, but he has a good grip of it, and at least he's not dropping it. She thinks of him across the ocean doing soldiering kinds of things, imagines him trying to load a rifle or a big cannon. This is how he will die. She can see his hands shaking at the wrong moment, see him drop an explosive, see his body blown into little cutlet pieces.

She wants to go to him now and tell him to hide from the men from the draft. She wants to tell him that they could run. At a word, she would leave with him for the desert, and when she gives him his lunch, she will tell him that. They could live out there where no one else is. She would survive on cacti and lizard tails if she had to. She would feed them to him if his hand were shaking too much, but she knows Eduardo and his code. She knows that he will go off to this war and die for these men or come back worse than he is now.

She wonders if John will still be waiting for her then. She wonders if he will be interested. She wonders if this second man would follow her even though it meant he winced and limped his way out to the desert, to find a place where they could have simple peace.

RINGTAILED DREAMS

In Ed's dreams, he's back to holding a rifle. He's aiming it across the field and pulling the trigger. Each time the man folds at the middle and collapses as though he started to genuflect to God and just kept going. Each time the man begins a screaming that does not end until Ed wakes up because the man he really did shoot screamed for hours and hours until finally his lieutenant slit his throat. Most nights, he dreams of that man.

When he wakes up in a sweat, he finds himself staring at the eyes of a ringtail sitting on the edge of the fires, looking not at any of the other men, only at him. He had a friend who tamed a ringtail. That man said that they owned a magic over the night. He said that they would wake you from bad dreams, and Ed thinks that maybe this one did.

"Thank you," he tells the little animal. He swears it's smiling at him.

"Shush." That's McMurphy, who he hadn't noticed was awake, who he hadn't noticed raising his pistol level with the animal's head. "You're going to scare it away."

"McMurphy," he says. "If you kill that little cat, I'm going to shoot you right in the stomach." It's the worst punishment that he can dream of.

He doesn't bother to turn to McMurphy, even though he knows the man is watching him. Instead, he keeps his eyes steadily on his magic friend. He can see into the animal. He can feel its joy.

THE VIEW FROM SIGNAL HILL

Tina doesn't want to go, but when the newscasters say that the Los Angeles riots are over, finally over, she and Jacob come out of her apartment for the first time in three days and walk up Signal Hill to look over the city and see what it has done to itself. From up here, the city is smoldering, lines of smoke coming up across the valley. Tina has the quick fantasy that they're communication fires, people sending up SOS smoke signals, and there is so much terror in this world that all those fires have formed a dark cloud above them and gloom all around.

She's brought out of her thoughts by a crack that she thinks is a gunshot at first. Jacob must too because he wraps her in his arms, gives her whatever protection there is in his body. Then, she feels his back tense, and in the e.s.p. of married people, she knows that it wasn't a gun, knows that he saw something, and it's all right.

"Are you out of your minds?" he yells.

She loosens herself from his arms and turns to see seven teen-aged boys. They're holding bottles and something else. It takes a moment for her to understand what they're doing, but she realizes they have fireworks, not guns.

They only glance up at Jacob, and they're back laughing joyfully with each other as though they're glad to be alive. She can't hear their words exactly, only that happy rumbling kids get when they're young. One lights a big firecracker, bigger than any Tina has ever seen and drops it in a bottle. He pauses a moment and lobs it in a high arc off the edge of the hill and toward the city. Somewhere on its downslope, the firecracker blows, sending glass shimmering down into the vacant lot below.

"Knock it off," Jacob yells. The anger is rising in his voice, making this deep-throated man nearly squeaky.

When Tina sees the look one of the kids give him, the deadness of eye and flatness around his mouth, she puts a hand on Jacob's shoulder. "Leave it alone."

Only, he's gone to his dark place. She's seen him disappear like this before. He'll lose himself in his anger and become so focused on it that he cannot hear anything else. Now, he shrugs her hand off his shoulder and takes a couple of steps forward.

"Go home," he yells at the kids.

"Fuck you, old man," one of the kids yells back. He's the one who just lobbed the bottle, and all of the others look to him first and seem to gain strength from his example.

"Knock it off. People are going to think they're still shooting."

The boys spread out in a line and come forward with the lead punk in the middle like this is West Side Story. They surround Tina and Jacob in a wide circle. The leader says, "You want to say something to me, old man?"

"Yeah." He steps forward, and Tina follows him. No stopping him now, but she wants to be close. "People have had enough of gunshots and explosions."

"People?" the punk looks around him as though he's looking for these people. He's a skinny little guy. He has that kind of sneer only teenaged bullies are able to achieve. "We're people, and we're not tired of it yet."

"If you don't stop it," Jacob jabs a finger at him, "they're going to call the cops. This neighborhood's had enough trouble."

The kid snorts a laugh. "They don't give a shit if we kill each other. The cops are all lined up protecting white people."

The thing about it, Tina realizes, is that the kid is at least half right. No cop is going to come, not for a couple of days probably. They're busy stopping real gunfire, or locking up people who looted in front of news cameras. They're making military looking formations in front of television cameras to prove they're bad-asses, or they're sweeping up glass with shopkeepers in front of cameras to prove they're good guys.

"Why don't we just leave?" Tina says.

"Yeah, man," the punk says. "Why don't you listen to your woman?" He steps forward, arms spread wide, sneer across his face.

He isn't making a move, but he advances toward Jacob like a playground bully. When he's a foot away, Jacob's right fist flashes and finds the middle of the punk's face. Tina can hear a popping sound and the kid, probably fifty pounds lighter and six inches shorter than Jacob, goes down on his back. When his friend comes forward, Jacob catches him on the side of the head with a left, and then the kids are running, all of them except for the two on the ground. From behind, they look like kids rushing out to recess, excited for fifteen minutes of unrestricted freedom.

"Come on," she says to Jacob. She grabs his hand and pulls him.

"What?" he says to the kid on the ground.

"Come on."

As she pulls him away, the kid looks hatred up at her man, and she wonders if this is the end or just the beginning of it. The world at this moment, with her city burning itself down, her man sweating and puffing his anger, this child bleeding from his face, she just wants to take Jacob and leave it. She wants to flee someplace no one would ever find them again.

If she could, she'd take Jacob and drive out to a little cabin in the desert where no one would bother them. She'd live as simply as she could. If they'd have to, they could live on cacti and lizard tails just so long as they could find a place of ease, someplace where there is peace.

PART THREE
I AM NOT FREE

"Your Honor, years ago I recognized my kinship with all living beings, and I made up my mind then that I was not one bit better than the meanest on earth. I said then, and I say now, that while there is a lower class, I am in it; and while there is a criminal element, I am of it; and while there is a soul in prison, I am not free."

— Eugene V. Debs

SANDRA WHO

In the mornings, Sandra, who lives in Pomona, draws the white people as they go to the medical school. She sits on her porch and sketches them walking, their heads facing forward, never at her. She wants to capture their movement, their drive, their passion on the way toward their dreams.

Sandra, who lives in Pomona, asks her mother if she can walk down to the medical school to sit on one of the benches and draw the people from a new angle, but her mother says that the medical school is no place for her.

"They would chase you out as soon as they saw you, Baby."

Sandra, who lives in Pomona, wants to call to one of them, ask them to pose. She wants to draw the face of success and hope. She wants to know what that looks like.

THE SORROWFUL MUSIC OF COWS

The tule fog makes the valley nearly unrecognizable to Harry who's been gone five years now. It used to be that he could drive these roads, pushing his old truck as fast as it would go, and he'd know where to turn because he'd see a familiar fence post or a tree. Today, he has to ask where to get off the bus, and when he walks the half mile to his parents' house, each thing he used to recognize seems changed. The houses are larger or smaller than they had been in his mind. That oak tree lied to his memory and is now a lemon tree.

A half block away from his parents' little white house, two cows solidify themselves out of the fog. Strays, of course, but they're standing comfortably on the front lawn staring at Harry as though he's the outsider. One of them moos at him unpleasantly as he passes. He tries the knob, but it's locked. Then he tries his key, but the lock has been changed, so he raps on the front door and yells, "Mom."

When he hears the sharp click of a woman's heels inside the house, he slicks back his hair and pushes out his best smile. Only, it's not his mother who opens the door, but a woman his age who swings the door wide and levels a shotgun at his middle.

Harry steps back without meaning to, stumbles off the top step of the porch, and trips nearly into one of the cows, but he keeps his feet. "Stephanie?"

They stare at each other for a long moment, Harry lost in that memory of her laughing and those years he would have done anything to make her his. "Your parents moved away. They sold me their house six months ago when they heard you were getting out."

Harry's eyes go down to the barrels. "Where did they go?"

"They left because they thought you might be coming. They told me not to give you their address."

Harry shakes his head. The fog, the cows, Stephanie now here in this strange world. None of it makes sense.

"I want you off of my property," she says. "I want you out of my life forever."

He thinks about that night, and almost doesn't blame her for the hatred tensing her shoulder muscles. "I'm sorry. You have to believe me. I was drunk."

She bites her lip in that way that she has. She's breaking on the inside, he knows. Still, she says, "Yeah, you were drunk, and now you're leaving. I'm not kidding."

"Come on. Even the State of California says that I've done my time."

"You might be square with California, but you'll never be right by me." She keeps the gun pointed at his center and slams the door with a quick, sweeping kick.

"Stephanie," he yells at the house, but the wall echoes his word back at him. He turns to the cow nearest to him as though she might have an insight here, but the old girl just stares blank wisdom into his face.

After a few moments, Harry cuts around to the back of the house to the tool shed. It's still there, thank god. This is the one bit of the Central Valley that hasn't seemed to change. He steps inside and gets down on his knees to pry open his secret floor board. Inside, his notebook waits for him. It's then he hears her step behind him outside of the little building.

"I don't know what you're doing in there, but come out now."

He turns around slowly, keeping a smile on his face and his hands above his head, the notebook in his left. "I want to leave," he says. "I just want to get out of your hair." He steps out of the little shack and into the fog.

"That's your one option, and you can leave that behind you."

"My notebook?"

"My notebook. When your parents sold their house to me, everything they left behind became mine."

Harry can feel the air being pulled out of his chest. "It's a diary. It's not even valuable or anything."

"Then why do you want it?"

He can feel the tears coming up the way they used to sometimes in Folsom. That was the place where he learned the twisted gift of keeping tears inside.

"I want it because," but he can't explain it out loud, not what it really means to him. "It's the only thing in the world that's really mine."

She scoffs a laugh. "That's not true," she says. "That notebook was Harry's. Harry died five years ago. You're the monster that took over his body." She nods her head to the ground. "You can put it down there."

"Please," he says, but she doesn't even bother to respond.

"Please."

She only shakes her head.

As Harry crouches down to leave that last part of his boyhood on the ground between himself and the woman whom he once loved, the cows in the front yard bellow, and it seems to Harry that the old girls are singing a mournful kind of song in this moment, a dirge to the man he once was.

THE FOUNTAINHEAD

JEFFREY, WHO drives for Mr. Newman, spends his afternoon reading a paperback outside the school Newman's boy attends. Mr. Newman gave him *The Fountainhead* to read as though he would have never heard of it before, as though this would be the revelation that would make him beg his employer to lower his salary. Because he knows the man, he knew to pretend to be surprised by the ideas, but he tossed the book out the window into a rain-filled gutter. Mr. Newman doesn't know that Jeffrey is in the American Communist Party. Not many people do.

When the bell rings, Jeffrey puts down his novel and watches for the boy coming through the gate followed by three other children. This is the moment he has been waiting for all day, and he opens his box of Raisinets. He laughs all the way through the beating, thinking of it as Karma in reverse for all the pain the rich little bastard will rain down on the poor when he grows up. This evening, he will listen at the door when his father scolds him for being beaten up. He will tell his boy that he needs to be self-sufficient. He will tell his boy that Newmans are so much better than that scum.

FIGHT OR FLIGHT

"Gonna be terminal?"

"Huh?"

"What's gonna be?"

"Pardon?"

"Terminal. What's gonna be terminal. You said it, not me."

August stops digging and takes off his hat without looking up. He pulls a kerchief from his trouser pocket and dabs at his thinning hairline. "A terminal. This is going to be *a* terminal."

Bud's expression does not change.

"As in Union Station," August stuffs the kerchief back into his pocket. And with that, he slams the shovel blade into the trench bottom and sniffs, then chuckles under his breath. "Terminal."

"Union what now?" Bud asks with a jut of his chin.

"Now you're just playin' with me—"

But Bud is perplexed. Clearly not the sharpest tool in the shed, August thinks. He sweeps his arm in front of him, as if introducing Bud to the world: "This. What we're working on here, it's all going to be the Union Station Terminal."

"Oh *that* kind of terminal! I get it now."

Ralph shakes his head.

"But, how do you know?"

"Man said it when he hired us."

"Didn't say nothin' to me," Bud says.

"He said it to all of us, there at the gate."

"Well, I don't much care what it is, just so long as their dollar's good."

"Yup," August says. "Just grateful for an honest day's work."

"You betcha. Diggin' post holes ain't so bad."

"Trenches," August corrects, slamming his shovel blade into the soil as if punctuating his sentence.

"Were you in the trenches?" Bud asks, tossing a shovelful of dirt into the pile to their right.

"Nope. Got discharged before they could ship me out."

"How'd you swing that? Musta had a friend as your Commanding Officer."

"Hardly. I punched my C.O. in the nose. Well, chin actually. Broke his jaw."

"Uh oh."

"Had it coming." Both men stop digging. "Sent him backwards down half a flight of steps. Thought I had killed him."

After a few seconds, Bud sniffs and says. "Listen. If I get out of line or piss you off, you just let me know. No need to resort to violence here."

August laughs now. "Oh, I'll give you fair warning."

CAPTURED

Bud slides across the hardwood floor and under the bed frame like Kiki Cuyler of the Cubs stealing second. In one motion, he slips his legs into the hanging leather harness, slides his arms into the matching loop near the head of the bed, as practiced hundreds of times for just such an occasion.

By the time the feds bust the front door open on their third blow, he has already pulled the window shade mounted sideways underneath him and latched it, so that anyone looking under the bed won't see him hanging.

When the footsteps reach the bedroom, he holds his breath. A matchstick flares as it scrapes the door jamb. Bud smells the burn of tobacco and rolling paper.

"Well, now. You seem all comfy cozy, Bud. Can I roll you a cig for the road?"

Bud squeezes his eyes tight in frustration.

"Ollie ollie oxen..."

Bud inhales as silently as he can.

"Now see, I would say 'free free free' but that would just be cruel, considering the circumstances. Seeing as how you're gonna be locked up for quite a while for all we got on you."

Bud opens his eyes.

"Been a while since I jumped up and down on a bed, but hell, looks like I got me some free time here." Agent Norman flicks his cigarette under the bed and leaps up onto the mattress, bouncing slightly. "Seems to have a bit of extra padding. Maybe a pea under this mattress, ya' think?" Agent Norman jumps once. The slats creak. "Or maybe a princess under there?" He hops up and down seven times, rocking Bud to the point his forehead is striking the box springs where his head bounces between the slats. The bedposts start lifting off the floor the higher Agent Norman jumps. The leather straps dig deeper into the back of Bud's thighs and armpits.

Then just as quickly, Agent Norman stops. "Uncle?"

"Uncle, you sumnabitch."

MARTY WAS HERE

Harrison concentrates on just breathing for a moment in his car outside of his apartment. It's been a long day, one that's ended with his son, Stanley, being committed for forty-eight hours, and he wonders, now that he doesn't have to deal with Stan yelling at him or staring out the window or trying to sneak out to buy alcohol only to have the police call him at three in the morning, what he's going to do with his evening.

A wave of relief washes over Harrison, and he pulls out his phone with the idea that he might call Bridget to see what she's doing, and this sense of relief is followed almost immediately by a new kind of shame that he never would have thought himself capable of. He wants to smash his fist into his steering wheel, yell and curse and maybe weep, and he would have sixteen years ago, but back then he wasn't the father of a boy. He had the freedom to have emotions and the sure knowledge that he could solve his and everyone else's problems, so instead, he rests his forehead on his hand for a moment to get his mind right. Back then, he could fix everything, at least what he was presented with, and somehow, he wishes he could just get back to that time.

Slowly, he becomes aware that the dog in the house across the street has been barking a long time now. Norman, Harrison thinks. He had a conversation with the owners once while Stanley stroked the dog and told him he was a good boy. That might have been the last time he saw his son have pure childlike joy. Harrison blinks twice and looks around. There's a foreclosure sign in front of the two-story house that he hasn't noticed until now. He wonders how long it has been there, if it went up today, or if he'd missed it because there are so many lately.

Then he realizes that the dog is back there terrified of something, and the house looks abandoned. The potted plants are gone. The welcome mat is missing. Harrison walks around to the side fence and spots the dog barking hopelessly into the dark sky.

The dog turns to Harrison, wagging his tail, but he doesn't come forward because he's on a chain that's wrapped itself around the bottom of a basketball pole. When Harrison opens the side gate and walks to him, Norman does a dog's dance of excitement with his forepaws. He's pumping his tail.

"Hey buddy," Harrison says. "Hey there." As he unclips the dog, he hears a click behind him from the house.

A man is standing in the sliding glass window staring at him, a short guy in jeans and a white shirt with his black hair slicked back, so Harrison stands and raises his hands. "Oh, God," he says. "I'm sorry. I thought everyone had left."

The man mouths, "What?" through the glass. He unlatches and opens the door.

"I'm sorry," Harrison says.

Only, the man doesn't seem to hear him. "I needed to get clean."

"I thought you'd left the dog. I didn't want him to choke himself."

The man stares at Norman for a long time. He turns to Harrison. "I didn't hurt him or anything. He was barking when I got here."

Harrison realizes something is wrong, but he's not sure yet what the disconnect is. "You're going to take him though, right? You're not going to just leave him."

"Take him? What's his name?"

"Norman," Harrison says, and he understands what's happening, who this man is.

"You're not going to call the cops or anything, are you?"

"I don't understand," Harrison says even though he does. He

can feel his voice getting deeper, the automatic adrenaline response in his body, making him stand taller. It's a million years of evolution working inside him to protect him from danger. His body has chosen fight.

"I'm not hurting anything. I have a job interview tomorrow. I need to get clean," the man says, his body apparently choosing flight.

"What are you doing here?"

"Can't you just let me get clean for the interview? It's at a big box store."

Harrison stares at him, not sure what he's supposed to do in this situation, what his role is.

"One night." Tears are beginning to creep into the man's voice.

Harrison can hear himself saying, "All right, I'll think about it." Why he imagines he has the right to make this decision is beyond him. "I'm going to take Norman for now."

"Right. Norman." He closes the glass door, but keeps his eyes on Harrison.

A half hour later, the dog is asleep on Harrison's couch as if he's lived here his whole life, and Harrison is playing those moments over for the tenth time, trying to push out the idea that in twenty years, Stanley will be just like this man. He stares out his window at the house and thinks about the kinds of people who have put themselves in between the man and happiness. Harrison is one of those people.

So Harrison goes into the closet, into the shoebox where he keeps his mad money, takes out two twenty dollar bills, weighs his guilt, and adds three more bills. He walks across the street, goes through the side gate, and taps on the sliding glass door, but there's no response.

He taps again, knowing that there never will be a response, so he pushes the door open, and says, "Hello."

The house has the unmistakable feeling of emptiness, but Harrison walks in anyway, his money held out in front of him the way a vampire hunter holds a cross. "Hello," he calls.

Nothing in the kitchen. No one in the living room, bedrooms, or bathrooms. No one upstairs or down. On the bathroom mirror on the ground floor, someone has written "Marty was here!" in black magic marker.

Harrison puts the money into his pocket and wonders if the man in the blue jeans is Marty or if it's one of the people who lost the home in foreclosure. He wonders who is going to take over this house, and if, when the bank sends the real estate people, they will see what Marty has written and understand it. He wonders if he understands it or the man, and he hopes he does, but he has a feeling that the man like everyone, like Norman, like Stanley, like Harrison, is completely abandoned in this world, screaming that they are here into a dark night that does not care.

THE LAST DAY OF MARCH

They repo Peter's car on the last day of March, so he doesn't really have anywhere to sleep, and since they take it while he's in the bathroom, they get everything but the clothes he has on and the money in his pocket, which is something, and at least he has his jacket. He could go to stay with his sister, but after the last time, he doesn't think she'll let him. Instead, he goes into the grocery and buys himself a fifth and wanders down to the beach.

This was what it was like in college, he decides. Back then, he'd go down to the beach with his friends and drink and watch the stars pop out one at a time. The only difference now is that his friends aren't here. He lost track of them somewhere along the line, but he likes to think of them, where they must be. Joey's a lawyer, two kids probably, and knowing him, divorced. He takes a sip. Carlos has to be a cardiologist, and maybe he's come out to himself by now. And Stephan is probably teaching children. He probably has ten of his own.

Peter loves the rhythm of the water and the way the bourbon burns the back of his throat. It warms him until the night is almost warmer than he can take. He thinks that after another drink or two he'll go for a quick swim. The way he's feeling now, maybe he'll swim all the way to Catalina and back.

A KIND OF SOCIAL JUSTICE

THEY HOLD Dale's retirement breakfast in the far corner of a ballroom on a Friday morning, forty-three people huddled together in a room meant for two thousand. That's all right, he supposes, as is the gold watch and the handshakes and sentiments, but he's happy to get out of there. When he does, he's surprised at the lack of sentiment he has for Continental Works, his boss, coworkers, and the profession of civil engineering.

Mostly what he thinks about as he drives through this neighborhood is how closely his life has stayed on the little path he thought it would take. His retirement party, after all, is in the town where he went to college. On a whim, he drives up to the old neighborhood in Claremont where he rented a backhouse, he and his three roommates, one of them the only black person he knew in the entire city.

He parks in front of the place and can see into the yard. The mother-in-law house they used to rent is gone, replaced by a giant pool. Across the street there is an open house, and Dale goes in. He's still wearing his suit and tie from the breakfast, and the woman who's selling it gives him a quick look and smiles broadly. "Hi, you in the market for a home?"

"No," Dale says without bothering to think about a lie. "I was in the neighborhood, and I was remembering a time when I broke into this place as a kid. I wanted to see if it had changed."

Once it's out of his mouth, Dale can hear how it sounds, wonders if he's scared the poor woman, but she cocks her head, shifts her weight to her other leg, and laughs. "Well, I've never heard that one before. What, are you just getting out of prison today?"

"No, it wasn't like that." Dale smiles. "It was a dare in college. I used to live with a black guy named Stuart. I was trying to prove to him that it wasn't any easier being white than it was being black."

The real estate agent laughs again. She knows how to do it so it doesn't feel fake the way he'd expect from someone trying to sell him a house. Maybe it is real, too. She leans against a doorjamb framing herself in front of a window onto the backyard. "Did you actually believe that?"

"Sure. I was young. There was a big party going on across the street, and he bet I could just walk in and no one would stop me, but they'd probably call the cops on him."

"And?"

"And they stopped him at the door."

"And you?" She folds her arms.

Dale shrugs. "I walked right in. It was a wedding reception, and no one had any idea who I was. I just put on a tie, and no one thought to question me. When Stuart came in, they did everything but call the cops."

"You're like me." She smiles at him. "You've had just one big indiscretion in life, right?"

"Yeah, but that's not the end of the story. I got a drink at the open bar and a steak, and I knew that Stuart had been right. I sat there talking to the bride's sister, who was feeling bad about her dress, and I realized that I could do pretty much anything I wanted in this house."

"You mean to her?"

He shakes his head. "No, not like that." He thinks a moment. "I guess maybe like that too. I mean if I wanted to. I realized that I walked around like I came from money, which I did, and that meant people looked at me differently."

"So what did you do?"

Dale can feel himself blushing. He's never admitted this part of the story to anyone in his life. "Well, I went into the bedroom where all the purses and jackets were, and I stole a couple hundred dollars out of a woman's wallet."

She covers her mouth with her hand. "Seriously?"

"I took Stuart on a road trip to Vegas and thought of it as a kind of social justice. The woman's purse was made out of expensive leather, and it was on top of a fur coat."

"So Stuart was right."

"Yeah, he was. I could have made a career out of breaking into houses if I had wanted to. I was thinking that now that I'm old and look like I come from money, I could have an entire second career of crime."

"Same holds true for me," she says. "People trust women more than men, but the thing about crime is that you don't make all that much money doing it."

"Second careers aren't about money really. They're about new experiences." He's joking. Of course he is, but there's something to what he's saying. "So what was your one big indiscretion?"

She laughs and waves a hand at him and blushes, and he's sure she's not going to answer, but she says, "I slept with a married man."

"Yeah?"

"I was nineteen, and he was a minister, and there was something really sexy about that."

"Were you married?"

She shakes her head. "No. I never thought about the other woman." She's been smiling this whole time, but it weakens now, wavers. "Oh, God, I've been thinking about her lately." She shakes her head and laughs a little to herself.

"And you've followed the rules ever since?"

"Sure," she says. "I never break the rules anymore."

"But you wish you had."

She shrugs. "No. I wish everyone had. I wish that the world were full of rule followers, but that's just not who we are. So I guess I might as well just break all the damn rules."

"Do you want to get back at him a little maybe? Maybe with me?" Dale knows there must be someone else, knows what he must have done. Still, Dale can't believe that he's saying this, Dale Worth, retired civil engineer, coming up with lines like this.

She must be surprised too because she looks at him in a way that women haven't in a long time. He must be exuding confidence. Maybe she has a bad boy thing. He hasn't been a bad boy since the day he broke into that house, and come to think of it, he got laid in Vegas that weekend a couple of times.

Whatever the reason, when she leads Dale back to the bathroom, it doesn't feel as if it's about him, but what does that matter? It's not about her either. It's about that terrible breakfast commemorating the last forty-one years. It's about what he might have been doing that whole time, what he's missed out on in his windowless office.

They have sex on the edge of a bathroom counter quickly, roughly, ending before anyone else comes to the open house. When they're done, they laugh together, not really because anything is funny. They just laugh. Her skirt is off but her blazer and blouse are still on, and that's funny to him now that he notices it. He laughs once more.

The bathroom seems to be a world to itself where the rest of society doesn't exist and rules don't apply. Inside, they are friendly partners, and she keeps her palm resting on his chest. When they leave, she turns into the aloof saleswoman, which is almost certainly the mask she wears for the world.

"So," she says, straightening her skirt, "I don't suppose there's any chance that you're actually interested in buying a house in

Claremont?"

"No." He shakes his head.

"Well then. Maybe in the future." She offers him a card that he takes and reads. Her name is Shirley.

This is the problem with crime, dangerous sex, theft, or whatever. The profits are never good unless someone really knows what he's doing. Dale tosses the card on the front stoop as soon as he closes the door, and he thinks about Stuart. At some point thirty-five years ago, they lost touch. By then, Stuart was an accountant who had moved to downtown Los Angeles. He wonders what happened to him in the riots of 1992. He wonders if life has gotten any easier for him, and if he has a family, and if he is rich.

Maybe he'll call him when he has time. Maybe he'll look up Shirley, too. Probably not. His wife is waiting for him with a little retirement party with his family. The kids. The grandkids.

For now, he has to get home.

A QUICK MOMENT OF TOM

On the week of Truman's wedding, Carrie's parents tell her that maybe she should take a trip. They'll send her anywhere she wants. Carrie, of course, wants to go to Hollywood, and leaving town, getting out of the state turns what might have been the worst week of her life into a kind of magic, and she sees the life that she still might have in the beaches and limousines, and with fancy people, a life that she would never have had with Truman.

Little magic things happen all week. She eats at the Derby. She meets a boy that she kisses, and she doesn't think about Truman for the entire time. She goes to Disneyland. She's down at the Farmer's Market the day before she's supposed to go home, thinking about whether she's going to stay or not when a man out of nowhere starts to shout that he's got free tickets to see Johnny Carson tonight. It stops her breath in her chest, and she's unable to move for a second, and then her reflexes take over because she knows that if she doesn't move right now all these people swirling around her are going to push her out of the way, and she's going to miss her shot.

Only, everyone must be asleep on their feet because she's over to the man taking his tickets before anyone else seems to notice what's happening. It's like she's won the lottery, and he even offers her more tickets for her friends, but no, there's only her alone on vacation. When she asks him who the guest star is, and he says Tom Selleck, she just about pees herself.

They film the show in the late afternoon, but she gets on the crosstown bus before lunch, just to make sure that she gets there in time. This whole trip has been like the dream that Tru said would never happen, but with Tom Selleck, it's like a message from God. Johnny and Thomas. Tom and John. Those were the names she and Tru had picked out if it had turned out to be a boy. She thought of the child as Tomorjohn before she lost it.

It's like God's giving her permission to dream again, and she knows what dream he's giving to her. It's the only one that makes sense. Tru always said that with her face she could never be a looker, but she had about the best boobs in the world. He said maybe she had a shot at the headless lingerie ads they put in catalogs and newspapers. It had been said as a mean joke, but she knew he was right, and she's treasured his words.

Since this trip has been so amazing, she allows herself to dream on the bus across town. Magnum P.I. himself sees her and recognizes her quality. Johnny Carson brings her up on stage. She has a kind of celebrity for being such a genuine and good person. She sees long lunches surrounded by people like Johnny and Tom. She drops witty remarks that make them smirk despite themselves. Tru's stuck back at home with his cow and their new brat while she's out here. She drinks champagne for breakfast, buckets of it.

Sitting at the back of the bus, she laughs at the thought of it, and then looks around to see if anyone noticed her, and no one seems to.

The only thing she can't see in her dream is how they meet, and this is fantasy, she knows that it is fantasy, but she tries to imagine it, and it slowly dawns on her that they keep passing men on the street selling flowers, and the idea, so simple and obvious overtakes her.

She walks up to the front of the bus and says to the driver, "Mister, I know you're not supposed to do this, but would you mind pulling over for a moment to let me buy flowers from one of those men?"

She points at a man they pass selling daisies out of a bucket.

The man, who looks a little bit like her father, turns and frowns at her. "What do you want me to do that for?"

She smiles, blushes at herself. "It's silly."

He looks her up and down, lingers maybe on her chest. "I'm not going to stop unless you have a damn good reason."

"Well, I'm going to the Tonight Show, and I want to give them to Mr. Selleck, who's the guest."

She'll send them to him, and he'll come out to thank her, and she'll tell him about the funny coincidence about Tomorjohn, her baby who died, and he'll laugh and bring her backstage to his dressing room. From there, what happens will happen. No use in planning that.

The man in the bus laughs and stares at her a moment like she's joking even though he's still driving at forty miles an hour. She wraps her arms behind her. Tru was right, after all, and why not use them?

"All right," he says. "It's not a good reason, but it's crazy enough."

She giggles at the providence of it all except the man behind her says, "Don't let her out here."

"Why not?"

The man, who's maybe fifty and in a suit, waves outside.

"It's Hollywood," he says, like that means something.

"She'll be fine," the woman sitting across from him says. She's doing a crossword but doesn't look up. "It'll be fine."

"You don't know what Hollywood's like. A little girl like you and you flash money? Don't let her out, driver."

"Maybe you're right," the driver says. Carrie gets a vision of Tom Selleck walking backward into a bank of fog, waving goodbye to her, so she bends over at the waist to lean over him. "It'll be all right," she says. "It's Hollywood. The worst that will happen to me is that someone will discover me."

The man takes off his reading glasses, lowers his newspaper, and stares at her. "Discover you doing what?" Then he seems to realize what she means because he says, "Oh" in a long breath, and then, "God, don't let her off this bus. They're going to eat her alive."

She looks out the window to see what he could possibly mean and sees a man who she thinks at first is staring at a wall in an alley but then realizes is peeing.

Still.

"I'm not going to be out there long. Just to get flowers."

The woman says, "Shouldn't there be some kind of Irving Berlin music starting now?" She doesn't bother looking up from the crossword.

"What?"

"You're supposed to say something like, 'Listen, Mister, I got dreams, and no one can stop a girl with dreams.'"

"What?"

"We have to protect her."

"Should I stop or not?"

"I been through my share of hard knocks, Mister, and now it's my time to shine."

"What?" At this they laugh.

"You came out here to be an actress?" The man with the newspaper says.

"No," she says. "I was thinking model." Tru had been right about this too. He'd seen her try and fall flat on her face at the school play. Everyone had. He'd told her she'd better rely on her boobs, and he'd been right.

The man says, "Let's see your stuff." He is in a business suit, and the way this trip has been going, he might just be in the industry. Still, he doesn't know what kind of model she wants to be. Does that matter out here? They say everything's different on the coast, more liberal and free. Should she show him?

She opens her mouth to speak, but nothing comes out.

"Listen Mister, I know I gots the chops to make it. I'm a looker."

She's not sure what exactly to say or how to show him her stuff, but she doesn't want to miss this moment, so she extends a hand. "I'm Carrie." He smiles slowly, shakes her hand back. "What's your name?"

He laughs. "What difference does it make?"

"I just want to know."

He rolls his eyes up like he's trying to think of a name. "I'm Lee Iacocca."

Maybe he is in the industry because she knows she's heard that name before. She has a quick flash of her and Lee sitting there with Magnum over sweet cocktails laughing. Everything smells like vermouth. They ask her to dance.

"God, leave her alone," the driver says, but Carrie sits down next to Mr. Iacocca.

He says, "You know, I think maybe you really should be a little more careful about where you sit and who you talk to."

She laughs, throws her head back, places a hand on his thigh, a hand that he lifts off his leg, and she blushes again and sits well back into her seat.

"Do you still want to stop for flowers?" the bus driver says. He points out the front window at a man with another bucket.

"Yeah," she says, and he does pull over, the nice driver. She hands the man five dollars and he hands her Magnum's bouquet of daisies, and she jumps back on the bus smiling at the driver. She wants to kiss him on the cheek, this man who looks a little like her father. He smells of Tru when he was going to take her out on a date. She thinks of that dream that she once had of her and Tru lying in bed with Tomorjohn between them cooing and they would be laughing. Only this dream is better, and it's so close now.

It's going to come together for her, this trip, and she's going to rise out of it all. Magnum and Johnny will see her breasts from across the crowded room, and they will know that she's the one who sent the nice flowers, only now she realizes as they pull away that she bought only one bouquet. One of them will be flattered and the other hurt. Still, that little bit of rivalry will mean that Johnny will bring her up on stage, and she will tell them the story of Tru and Tomorjohn and they will all laugh at Tru for missing his chance, and that makes her want to laugh.

It's all so beautiful that she wants to cry. She could break down weeping. Right here on Hollywood and Vine.

SQUARE NAILS

In China, when she was Ahn, people said that she had a gift for nails. She practiced all she could, shaping and painting and making hands beautiful, and when she was good enough a man told her that she could move to Los Angeles and work and become rich.

In Long Beach, the man changes her name to Ann, and puts her to work in a line of women. He provides her with an apartment that she shares with five others and with food that tastes a little like home, and once a week, he lets her use a computer to send email messages, and with her plane tickets and everything else, it seems that no matter how many nails she paints, she is always behind.

He tells her that she does not have to be poor forever. He tells her that if she wants, she can sleep with men for money, but she does not want to. "The choice is yours," he says, and he shrugs.

In a month, her expenses have piled up, and she owes him thousands of dollars. In a year, he says that she owes him close to one hundred thousand. He says that not only she owes him but that her family owes as well.

The women who sleep with men tell her it's not as bad as she imagines. They tell her it's really nothing, and since she has a gift for nails, she is certain to have a talent for love as well. Her passion is obvious. It sings to the world through her fingertips.

ALLISON

When she arrives in the apartment in Oakland, they change her name to Allison, and tell her that she should forget what her parents and friends had called her in Vietnam. They are dead to her. She is dead to them. Vietnam is dead. The East is dead, its food, its religion. All of it is dead, and she puts all of that away in a room in her head so she can play to the needs of the men who come to the house. These men who fought for her people and against her people in her homeland, come to her hungry, and watch her with need in their eyes. It was the same there. Back then they searched for an escape from the war. Now they want to escape back into the war. When a man likes her and comes back to her again and again, and when he asks her if he could get her something, a little token, she always asks for colored paper. When she likes that man too, she will make him a little animal out of that paper to remember her with. She calls them her little monsters. They escape this world for her. They find their way into the nice homes of men who live the secret life of need.

MARTHA WHO

Martha wakes up still bourbon dizzy from last night. The light is streaming through his window, and she knows that she's pushing it, knows that there will be no acting contract or even a bit part if his wife comes home and finds her in bed with him, so she dresses quietly and walks out into the street, wondering exactly what street it is.

The light, she decides is a kind of Burbank light, which isn't the same thing as a Beverly Hills light, but it's going in that direction, and she sits down on a bus stop just trying to get herself together for a moment, when she notices his wife walking past her and going up into the apartment, her bags heavy from her trip to Paris, that look of confidence on her face that says she's the type of woman who goes to Paris.

The thing is that his wife is beautiful. Martha kind of loves her. Today, she decides, everything is beautiful, the light streaming through the spring leaves, the cars rushing by on whatever street this is, and her whole future. It's laid out perfectly before her. The wild times and the wealth and all those people who will love her once they see her on camera. The main thing is that they love her, the way he loved her last night, and probably will in the future. Love is what makes a thing beautiful, so she decides that she must love his wife, and that feels right. That's what gives this moment so much joy.

PART FOUR
A THINKING ANIMAL

"Excellence is an art won by training and habituation. We do not act rightly because we have virtue or excellence, but rather we have those because we have acted rightly. We are what we repeatedly do. Excellence, then, is not an act, but a habit."

— Aristotle

THE WATER HUNTER

When Mary wrinkles her nose at the dinner table, her mother tells her that things are going to be different now that her father has gone off to basic training. They won't have enough money, and she doesn't know when he'll be back. She doesn't even know whether he's going to Germany or Japan yet. They're going to have to make their own way.

Early the next morning, Mary goes into the shed where her father keeps his hunting rifle and shells in a big oak box. It's padlocked, but she unscrews the hinges and takes it through the forest to the other side of the reservoir where no one ever goes.

It's the wrong kind of rifle for ducks. She knows it is, but she takes her time sighting a big white one floating near the shore. On the way home, she gets a rabbit too. She sees a deer and aims knowing that she won't pull the trigger because it's too big to carry home on her own.

Two years ago, when her mother told her how to plant potatoes, she cut up one for seed and planted it kind of as a game on the bank of the reservoir. She'd forgotten about that until now, forgot to see if she'd played her game well. It takes her a while to find her plant because the reservoir is low, but after some hunting, she finds them. They've mostly been gnawed apart by animals or bugs, but there are a couple worth taking, and maybe more under the ground.

When she comes home, her mother asks her where she got the duck and the rabbit. "I took dad's gun. He spent all last year teaching me how to shoot and clean it." She shrugs. "I thought I could help out a little."

Her mother frowns at her. Not angry. Thinking it through. "I don't know that your father would want you to do that."

"He told me I could if I wanted to. He said that if things start to get rough I should use it. That's why he taught me to shoot."

"You don't have a permit."

"I'll go out back through the woods so the police won't see me."

"You don't point it at anything until you know it's an animal."

Mary nods.

Mary gets meticulous, decides to spend a week figuring out the patterns of the patrolmen in the area. She and her mother are way back and out of town, so the policemen don't usually drive out this way, but she finds out the big yellow-haired cop drives the reservoir road at eight in the morning most weekday mornings, and the brown-haired cop with the moustache drives by at five in the evening.

It's easy. Another game for her, and her father has enough shells in his oak box for months and months. Her mother begins to hum again when she's fixing dinner. Mary takes the gnawed bits of potato out of the ground and replants what she can, thinking they'll have a crop in a few months. In a couple of weeks when the rains come again, she replants them higher on the hill. There's no knowing how full the reservoir will get.

Most mornings, Mary goes out to the banks of the reservoir before dawn to see the sun come up. She sits in the tall grass watching across the water, waiting for the yellow-haired cop to drive by. When he does, she smiles because she's won her game for the day. She picks up her father's rifle to find what she can.

It's five months before the soldiers come to tell Mary and her mother that her father has been shot by a German. "Where?" she asks.

The soldier narrows his eyes. "I don't know, but it was fatal."

"No, I mean where in Germany?"

"Oh," the soldier smiles at his misunderstanding and then becomes grave again. "In the countryside in France. A lot of men have died there."

After they leave, Mary's mother lies on her bed to weep, but Mary takes her father's gun, her gun, and walks to the reservoir. She sits on the shore all night watching the birds flitting about. She draws a bead again and again but doesn't shoot.

In the morning, she's still awake, and she's forgotten all about the yellow-haired cop, but there he is in his patrol car, driving across the water from her.

Mary sights him, and follows him with an invisible line between her eyes, her barrel and the side of his head. She breathes out as she aims, just as her father told her to. She thinks about the French countryside and the pictures she's seen of it in the library and the newspaper. She thinks about how much her father would have loved to see those French fields. Because her father would have wanted her to, she says, "Hail Mary, full of grace, the Lord is with thee. Blessed are thou among women, and blessed is the fruit of thy womb, Jesus. Holy Mary, mother of God, pray for us sinners now and at the hour of our death, amen." She keeps her aim until the yellow-haired cop turns the corner, and she knows that she doesn't believe in God any longer.

When he's gone, she places the rifle down in front of her and walks up the hill to tend to her potatoes. She leaves it there when she walks home.

All that winter, it snows in the mountains. All that summer, the snowmelt fills the reservoir. Mary watches the water creep towards the rifle she's left, every morning as she takes care of her potatoes. She plants squash, beans, and onions too. By the time she is sixteen years old, the rifle is hidden under the current, a secret that only she and the water know.

ACTS OF SELF-DESTRUCTION

On Tuesday morning, Eric Strege gets an insurance settlement for his daughter's death, two years after the fact. He never asked for it and doesn't want it, but the hospital lawyers paid out. On Tuesday afternoon, he cashes the check and piles the money, fifty thousand dollars, into his glove compartment. He goes down to a bar and gets drunk for the first time he can remember since college, toasting Samantha to men who probably think he's talking about a girlfriend. What does it matter? He tips the bartender $1000 and picks a fight that he loses, but the cops don't show up, which he realizes was the point to begin with.

He wakes up Wednesday morning in his car and turns on his phone to find that Christy has been calling him all night. He calls her and says he's going to need a couple of days to himself, gets on the freeway, and drives.

He has no destination really, but in a few hours, he knows that he's headed toward San Diego. Or is it Mexico. In the end, it doesn't matter because when he pulls over for gas, he sees a man standing on the side of the road with a cardboard sign that says, "Hungry." Eric pulls over to him, close enough to smell the sweat and alcohol, close enough to see the dirt caked into the lines of his face. When he holds out five twenties, the man takes a step back as though Eric might bite him, and he says, "I don't understand."

The car behind Eric on the freeway off ramp honks, but he flips the guy off. "It's money," he says.

"I don't get it."

"I'm going to get some food. You want to come?"

The man tucks the cash in his pocket. "I'm not going to have to do anything, am I?"

Eric doesn't get the feeling that having to do something is necessarily a deal breaker. "Nah," he says. "I'm just hungry, and I don't want to eat alone."

The man, whose name is Alex, directs him to his favorite restaurant in this town that is not quite desert, not quite city, halfway to Nevada and halfway to Mexico. It's a pizza place he comes to when he gets enough cash, but Eric stops by the liquor store first.

When they get inside the restaurant, he orders a pitcher of beer, three pizzas, four orders of fried chicken legs, three orders of potato wedges, and a diet cola.

"That seems like a lot of food," Alex says.

"Oh shit. I forgot." He orders Alex a diet cola too.

The food comes, and he waits until no one is looking to pour a pint of bourbon into the pitcher of beer. The two toast each other, but Alex is watching him like something might be up. It doesn't stop the man from feasting on all of this orange food. He makes grunting noises as he gnaws, and it would bother Eric except he's making them too, and gulping his boilermakers loudly and more often.

It seems like an impossible job, but like Roman senators they finish their food and lean back. By this time, Eric is aware that people in the place are either watching them or pointedly not watching him, but what does he care? For the most part at this time in the morning, they are all employees getting ready for the lunch rush, and as long as he's paying, they work for him.

"You want to get out of here, Alex?" He drains his glass.

"Maybe you shouldn't be driving right now."

Eric tilts his head at the man's accent. "Are you from Texas?"

"Maine," he says. "Maybe let me drive you."

"You're in no better shape than I am."

He gets up and fishes out his keys. Outside, Alex says, "Then let me get you to a hotel."

It actually doesn't sound like a bad idea. Room service, maybe a pool. He could trash the place like he's a rock star from the 1970s.

Alex tries to take him to a cheap fleabag joint, but Eric doesn't even pull into the parking lot. "Isn't there a big Indian casino around here?"

"Sure," Alex says, and he takes him there.

He checks in, and Alex gets a shower. Eric wants to clean up as well after a night of sleeping in his car and two days of drinking, but he thinks better of it and goes down to the slots, where his new friend watches him win $1199 in the slots in a half hour.

"That's a good payday," Alex says. "Now's when you stop." He grabs Eric by the shoulder and pushes the button that makes the receipt come out of the machine. Eric misses the days when coins would clink out and make a big racket.

"Alex, how would you like $1199?"

The man lets his hand drop off Eric's shoulder and stares at him for a long moment. "Not if it means that I have to keep watching you kill yourself."

Just like that, the air is sucked out of Eric. These last twenty-four hours have been the first time in his life that he's ever lost control and now he has to hold on to a slot machine to keep from falling. Maybe he should have lost control earlier. He doesn't know, but the memory of all of it draws him into himself, and he knows that his little rebellion of self-destruction is over.

"Take the money, Alex. I'm going upstairs to get a nap."

He half-expects Alex to stop him and tell him to keep his money and give him some profound message of hope, but by the time he's in his room upstairs, he's realized that Alex isn't some kind of angel come down to change his life. He's a man who will probably take that money and spend it badly, make mistakes that can't be changed and ruin himself, just as Christy did when she married him, just as the doctors who treated Sam did, just as Eric has been doing his whole life.

THE TRAIN WHISTLE

While the bruises on her face and body heal, Sarah tries to figure out what she should do. She could take the pistol and shoot him or go to live with her parents, but she'd hang for the one, and her parents would just send her back for the other.

On the third day she remembers the train. Five years ago, a woman could have lit out on a horse, but a man like Colin would catch her in a day or two, and that would have just made things worse.

When he goes out at noon for a drink with all the big men in town, she takes the money she's hidden and the money he keeps in the desk. She puts all of her jewelry and his mother's rings into a bag, the pieces he planned to give to his sister. She doesn't even bother to pack a bag. She can buy what she wants at whatever her stop will be.

Her heart finally stops racing in the desert, and when she hears the train whistle, she laughs. To her, it's like the far off noise of people cheering, that moment when the sounds of all those people yelling together blend into a single triumphant call of joy.

THE WORLD GONE TO FLAME

WHEN TERESA is seven months pregnant, Samuel has to report to his submarine, which goes deep and out of contact as far as he's concerned. He dives into a place that he imagines as light blue. It gets so cold down there he and everyone else assume they've dived under the arctic icecap, and he thinks of light filtered through a glassy ceiling, though he knows it's probably just pitch black outside.

When he comes to port six months later in San Diego, it's to a world that has caught on fire in the late California summer, and he thinks about Teresa living as she does near the weeds on the far side of town. He wonders if the fire has burned down her apartment, if he still has a place there and if the child, boy or girl, looks anything like him. His best friend on the boat has bet him a hundred bucks that the kid won't.

On his motorcycle driving across town, for the first time Sam hopes that the child is actually his, and this feeling surprises him. It means him settling down one way or another, which is what he's been afraid of for he doesn't know how long, but as long as that means more than just child support payments, he can see himself as the father. He can see baseball games and picnics when he comes to shore, regular sex and lawn care, all that bullshit old guys seem to love. He thinks maybe he's going to love it too, but then he's always been a romantic.

The closer he gets to Teresa's neighborhood though, the closer he gets to the wildfire. Someone on base has told him has been going for five days. He thinks about Teresa and the kid burning to death, and then he thinks of Teresa and some other guy evacuating to a fleabag hotel together, the guy telling her things like, "Sam's never been there for you, Baby, but I will be."

It's true too, which makes it so much worse, and he finds himself choking the throttle of his bike and lane splitting down a jammed freeway at eighty miles an hour until he gets to her exit, and it's been blocked off by the cops. He argues with one of them, but no one's driving into this neighborhood. Instead, he goes two exits down, drives his bike as close as he can, parks, and slips past the cops down an alleyway so he can walk it to her place.

Half an hour later, he's unlocking her door and letting himself in and realizing that if the rest of town is evacuated, she's not going to be sitting here waiting for him.

Still, once he sees the picture of the baby boy on her refrigerator, he knows the walk was well worth it. The kid has brown eyes. He laughs. Yeah, he has brown eyes too. It's like proof almost. Close enough anyway.

He's got the picture of the little guy in his hand and laughing to himself especially since there's no other guy's picture on the wall when he hears a cop's voice, unmistakably a cop despite the fact that she's a woman, yelling outside the door. "Hello? Is someone in there?" There is that cop knock on the door, the four raps they do with a night stick.

Sam finds himself wiping tears out of his eyes that he didn't know he could ever have, and he tries to call back to her, but he can't seem to find his voice. "Hello? Come to the door right now."

"It's me," Sam calls, although he doesn't know what he means by that. "I'm in here."

"Sir, I'm going to need you to exit the apartment."

Sam does, keeping the photograph of the kid in a high chair in his hand, holding it out in front of him as though it explains everything. He opens the door and steps out to see the woman cop, a little blonde with her hand resting on her pistol, waiting for him on Teresa's parking spot.

"It's all right," he says. "I live here." The fire's back on the other side of the apartment, someplace up the hill that runs behind it. He can't see it yet, but he can smell it. It seems hotter here, but that might just be his imagination.

"Two problems. The first is the mandatory evacuation has been in effect for four hours. The second is that I know the woman who lives here. She and I are friends, and you don't live here."

"I used to. We're kind of on a break or something."

The cop's face softens. She bites her lower lip breaking the hard-as-nails kind of effect that she had going up to this moment. "So are you Jacob or Samuel?" she asks. She leaves her hand on the butt of her gun.

Sam can feel the air leaving him. "Samuel," he says. "Who's Jacob?"

In a flash, the softness is gone. She is no longer a woman. Just a cop. "That's not for me to say, Sir."

"Who's Jacob?"

The wind shifts and blows smoke in their direction and Sam turns around and backs up to see the flames cresting the hill above. "We have to get out of here," the cop says.

Before she can enforce what she's said though, there is a sound like marching, and the two of them turn to see a line of cows, seven of them, trotting down the middle of the deserted street and past them in the swirling wispy smoke.

"Sir, we have to leave. Now."

Somehow though, Sam can't take his eyes off the cows that are headed toward a line of police cars. Fire fighters maybe. He wonders if they'll think it's a stampede. If they'll shoot to kill.

"Sir!"

"I'm not leaving. This is my home, and I'm going to stand and fight for it." He can hear the petulant childishness in his voice.

He doesn't care.

"Sir. If you don't move, I'm going to arrest you right here." The wind is blowing embers and the fire is staring to flow downhill, almost like it's a liquid.

He can see that the tidal flood of flames is going to swoop around them soon, but he says, "You don't leave your home. You don't just abandon it."

She steps over to him and takes his arm gently with her hand. "Samuel. We have to get out of here while we can." She pulls at him.

"You're her friend?"

"A little. I moved here two months ago. I've been over a couple of times."

"She's talked about me?"

"Enough that I know your name."

"The boy." He shows her the picture. "Is he mine?"

"That's really not for me to say," she says, but he can hear something in her voice.

"What's his name?"

She pauses a moment even though he can see how much she just wants to run. "Well, she calls him Jake Junior."

With that, Sam feels all the energy drain out of him. He feels her tugging him, and now, he doesn't resist. She pulls him to her police cruiser, puts him in the back. Behind him the wave of flame is coming down toward the apartment, but the fire department is rushing toward it. Either they will save it or they won't. He supposes that's none of his concern.

Still, he has the picture of the baby in his hand, his baby as he thinks of him. He'll name the boy Trevor, maybe. Maybe he'll call the child, Little Sam.

BUFFALO SOLDIERS

E<small>D LIKES</small> it up on top of Mt. Whitney. He likes the work to get here, the trail that he and his Buffalo Soldier squad have cut up the side of the mountain. On one side, there are giant trees down below them. The other side is the desert out toward Death Valley and beyond. Here is a place of peace between the life of the forest and the death of the desert.

Ed thinks about the war in the Philippines, the bullet that took his left ear. He thinks about his father who was born on a plantation. He thinks about the work he's done in the army, and what he'll be asked to do once he leaves this posting in the mountains.

He thinks for a moment what it would be like if they, all of them, stepped off the edge of this mountain, what it would look like to see them floating down to earth, what that would sound like. He thinks of never taking another beating. He thinks about what people would say. He thinks about the beauty of that one moment even though he knows he would never take that step himself. He knows that the memory of this dream will stay with him, this beautiful floating moment will be his private gift to himself.

THE KILLER OF MEN, THE KILLER OF TREES

ED SLIPS one afternoon on base and tears open his leg so badly that he's discharged from the military, no longer a Buffalo Soldier and a black man with a limp on top of it. He lost an ear in the army. He lost a finger too, fighting in the Philippines. When he thinks about his career, the only part he truly loved was when he was guarding the giant Sequoia trees in the summer of 1904, so the Saturday after he's discharged, he limps his way out of San Francisco headed east searching for work.

A month later, the work he finds is on a logging crew, working for Harmon, a man who fought in the Philippines too, not that Ed ever knew him. He's an old guy, one of those ex-soldiers who thinks the war is still on. He tells Ed when he hires him that he'd never add him to his crew, but he's got too few men.

Ed gives him a soldier's "Yes sir," thinking this might get him in good with the boss, but Harmon laughs, shakes his head.

Ed should have known better, should have known what Harmon thought of negro soldiers.

The first week he's there, Ed's put on the crew with everyone else chopping down one of the giants. It takes a week. The men work all day and then sit nearly silently at night. Ed doesn't feel much like talking to anyone, feels like maybe he should grab a rifle and stop all of this, cutting down the trees he spent a year guarding and patrolling. He wonders what Colonel Young, his old C.O., would say about this. He wonders what he would have said about it if someone told him he'd be doing it.

Only, he doesn't have a gun.

When Harmon comes up to the camp, he finds himself alone with the man for a moment staring up at the tree. "What are they going to do with it?" he asks.

Harmon jumps a little, surprised maybe that Ed would talk to him, and normally he wouldn't, but he's heard something, and he wants to make sure.

"With what?"

Ed nods at the tree. "I heard they use the wood for toothpicks mostly."

Harmon looks hard at Ed for a long moment until Ed turns his eyes down.

That's the moment he decides he's going to kill the man. Gun or no gun, he's going to find a way, and then he's going to disappear into the forest. Who knows these mountains better than he does? Even with a limp, maybe he has a chance.

He starts to keep his eyes on the boss man during the day and at night. What he needs is a moment alone with him and an axe or a knife. Night would be the best, but that night, Harmon bunks with the white men. Ed takes a long knife and watches the fabric edge of the tent cabin. He doesn't know how many days Harmon will stay in camp. He doesn't know if he has the time to plan his murder or not.

The men spend all the next day hewing at the giant tree and eventually they knock the thing over, it falling slowly at first and crashing onto the ground with the sound of a cannon, cracking into pieces the size of small houses, shattering like a giant eggshell, and Ed would have expected yelling and whooping at such a moment, but they all watch it like they're tired.

When it's stopped moving, he walks to one of the giant cracks, and puts his hand into the stream of water flowing out of its side. The water is ice cold and Ed wonders why. He tastes it but it's bitter. Someone tells him the tree's probably older than Christ. Someone says that it's going to make a hell of a lot of toothpicks. That same man spits.

Harmon walks around the tree, and when he comes to Ed, Ed says, "Mr. Harmon."

"What?"

"I quit."

An hour later, Ed's waiting on the road he knows Harmon will take to walk down into the valley. Twelve hours later, Ed slits the man's throat. The blood that flows out of his neck is warm. He drags Harmon off the road and over the ridge. He drops the body off the side of a cliff, not that it will do much to help him.

Ed figures he has a day's head start, maybe two days before they send the trackers. Maybe Ed will lose them in this forest. Maybe not. He knows that he will never see these trees again, and he's all right with that.

This world was never made with the idea of Ed in it. There is no place for Ed in a world where they cut down the giant trees.

"REMEMBER WHEN WE GET THERE, HONEY..."

THE OLD man stares out at the water, remembers the night he spent alone in the woods, freezing and hungry, the vision of the wounded doe forever burned onto his memory as regret. He had fallen asleep at last under a pile of dry leaves for warmth, wishing he had shot himself instead. But after the rangers found him shortly after dawn and his father beat him with the sides of his fists until his lips split, he was wishing he'd shot his father instead.

For two years in a row following that trip, his father refused to celebrate his birthday. When he gave in on his seventeenth birthday, all he had said was, "Happy Birthday, boy. The doe died suffering, thanks to you."

The smell of wood smoke now brings the old man back to the moment. He is surprised to find himself standing by himself in the sand.

He looks around to see that the onlookers have moved down the shore, following the buck and the swimming lifeguards as the current pushes them all north. He looks back the other way to see his wife standing off by herself, thirty yards to the south. She has laced her fingers and is clutching them against her chest, her eyes closed, her head tipped down.

The sand makes his strides awkward, and his breath becomes labored, but with each step toward her he loves her more. By the time he reaches her side his growing smile bursts into a laugh, his eyes full and flashing. "Chula!"

She turns startled, and wonders who the strange man is and why he is about to cry. She wants to help him, but she is afraid.

He smiles and wipes his running nose with the back of his hand. "C'mon, ma. Let's go."

She smiled, the fear lifting with a gust of wind, and she allows the man to take her by the arm.

He starts to sing loudly. "I'll... beeee... down to get ya' in a taxi honey, better be ready by a half-past eight..."

She smiles and blushes as he leads her to the crowd, standing gathered at the shoreline.

She feels warmer but wonders why they are there. Her legs hurt. Her hands. She wonders if they are going to eat soon, and if her mother is still waiting for her at the store. The clouds are beautiful, but the wind, it is too cold, and she has to get back and fix the baby breakfast. She has always loved the sky at sunrise.

FERDINAND, LINCOLN, McKINLEY

For his fourteenth birthday, Carl gets a .22 rifle that he takes down to the bottom of his father's orange grove to the creek to shoot rabbits. It's a fog day. That's what his mother calls days when the fog rolls through the Central Valley and cuts them off from the world of people. On days like these, he likes to walk out here and listen to the sounds of the valley cutting through the soup and guess what they are.

He hears one automobile today. Maybe a Model T working its way through the little road that crosses the potato field below his father's place. Carl tries to guess where the vehicle is by its sound and then fires a shot, listening afterward in case he hit. In a moment, he decides he didn't and laughs, in part out of relief.

Carl kills three rabbits by the creek, and he's going to bring them home for dinner when he hears voices coming up the road. People walking, but he can't understand what they're saying so it sounds a little like water splashing over rocks. He raises his rifle and tries to guess where they're coming from. He sits, thinking about their voices and how the road turns. In a moment, he knows why he can't understand them, that they're speaking Spanish, and he pulls his trigger.

The .22 makes just a little crack sound compared to his father's weapons, but for a moment that noise is all there is, it fills the valley and the fog around him seems to be soaked in it. Then there is a silence that he uses to grab his rabbits by the ears, to slip into his father's orchard. The voices on the road start up again, and Carl lies down flat against the earth and behind the third row of trees in the fog dark.

No one has been hit. He knows that from their voices, but they're wary. "Hola!" he hears one yell, but he doesn't respond or move. He thinks about the assassin who killed the Archduke, whatever that is. He can't remember the man's name. He thinks of John Wilkes Booth. He thinks of the guy who shot McKinley.

The men come out of the fog like shadows at first, and Carl draws a bead on them. They're walking up to his father's place of course. Looking for work, probably. If he pulled the trigger now, put a bullet into the middle one, he could always say he'd been hunting rabbits and hadn't heard them. This would be an accident. They'd take away his gun, and maybe his father would have to pay the man's family something, but it wouldn't be too bad. The worst of it would be no more gun.

As they come out of the shadows and turn into actual men, he licks his lips at the excitement of it. He could do it now, while they are walking in front of him on the road just fifteen feet away. He takes a long breath and considers a plan.

LILY LIVER

Every year George pleads for his father to take him hunting for his birthday, and every year his father tells him he's not yet man enough. Six days before his fourteenth birthday George asks him again as they sit down to dinner. When his father says nothing, George adds, "Please, father," then deliberately smooths the thin black hairs on his upper lip with his fingertips, hoping his dad notices the hint of the moustache he's been trying to grow.

"This meatloaf sure is good," his father says at last. George sighs and drops his hands to the table, nearly tipping his water glass.

His father looks at him flatly, then across to George's mother. "Bake another meatloaf on Thursday, dear. Then make some sandwiches out of it so's me and the boy can take 'em on our hunting trip over the weekend." Then he shifts his gaze to the gravy boat and adds, "Pass the gravy, boy."

George looks quickly to his dad, then to his mom, who is smiling at him. He looks back to his dad, who finally looks back and winks. "I told you to pass the gravy, boy."

Later that evening his father presents him with the old Winchester Model 70 that he had shot his own first deer with when he was George's age. Over the next few weeks his father teaches him the protocol for handling a firearm, how to disassemble it all the way to rows of parts on the table, how to clean each piece, where to place oil, and how to put it all back together. A ritual, like church. And just as somber.

His father makes him promise he will practice every day so that he'll be able to do it all by himself, and says has to show him that he knows how before he can go.

"I can do it blindfolded. So you should be able to with both eyes open, right boy?"

So George practices every day, first disassembling the rifle completely, then putting it back together, loading the .257 Roberts whitetail shells, taking target practice at tin cans. And every day he imagines the cans are deer hearts, that he's killed his first buck, and over dinner he talks about how he hopes he can bag a ten-pointer on his very first day. Every night he prays for God to make it so.

And sure enough, the first hour of the first day God must had been listening to him all those nights because a ten-pointer bolts out into the clearing upwind and stands there, full profile, just waiting to be taken down.

George hears the hot whisper of his father from behind, "For Christ's sake would you look at that." Then closer to his ear, and barely audible, "Get him in your crosshairs, boy."

He fumbles for his rifle and shoulders it, but his hands are shaking.

"Don't think. Aim and pull."

George struggles to hold the deer's heart in center of the scope, but now his arms are jerking, and his throat tightens.

"He's going to sense you. Shoot him now, boy." His dad whispers.

He knows he hasn't crossed-haired him true, but George pulls the trigger anyway and the shot transforms the woods into something else, some other place, like when he enters the reservoir after leaping off the quarry cliff—a world of calm exploded into chaos in an instant. His feet start tingling, as if asleep, and the right side of his head is ringing. The smell of powder begins to bring the sound of the day back, and his father's voice is the first word of his new life: "Christ."

George looks up, but the buck has disappeared into the brambles, which seem to be rustling. Or maybe it's the breeze. George can't tell.

His father slaps the back of his head, hard. "Go find him. Or else."

George tracks the buck, or pretends to. There's no sign to follow. No trail of blood. Not one hoof print. His father walks behind him, wordless, the air heavier each hour as the sun climbs and the shadows shorten. By noon, George is sweating and light-headed and his left eyelid starts twitching. His stomach is gurgling and growling too, and he knows his father hears it, but they both remain silent. When George stops to look around, his father stops, five paces behind him. Whenever George looks to his father, his father turns his head to look away, or looks at his shoes, as if impatiently waiting. They go on like this, all afternoon, right until nightfall without a break, skipping the meatloaf sandwiches in their packs, which in the days prior George had imagined eating with his father over laughter and conversations about what a good day it was.

When the woods suddenly open out into a high meadow, his father stops and sits down on a rock. When George notices the conspicuous lack of boot crunch behind him, he turns to see his father sitting, staring at him.

"Ten-pointer..." The first words his father has said since they started tracking. His father shakes his head and pulls out his sandwich, unwraps it and starts eating.

Even though he's hungry, the deepening of the boy's shame makes his own sandwich tasteless. Each forced swallow hurts as it competes with the lump in his throat. Then, there in the blue mist of mountain dusk, standing alone in the middle of the meadow, he spots her. A beautiful cream-speckled doe, nearly adult. Not the ten-pointer. But a chance at redemption.

His father swings his gaze to where George is looking and sees her then, too. "Now," he whispers. "And don't miss."

George slowly reaches to his rifle on the ground, picks it up, moving his arms only a few inches each second. He feels a gust on the right side of his face. They are upwind. Good. But then his hands start to quiver again, and he tries to stop the tears from welling, but he can not. The boy lowers his rifle, sobbing silently, his shoulders shaking.

His father walks over in a crouch and kneels beside him. "If you can't even kill a scrawny doe…"

But the boy's face is bright red. His eyes plead.

"One way or another, the doe drops by the count of ten. You man enough or not?" he whispers.

The boy's eyes flash, lost, and he looks somewhere over his father's head, as if something were there in the sky, but the boy sees nothing.

"I'm going home with that doe. Whether I go home with a son is up to you, you lily liver—"

The open-handed slap brings George back into the awful moment, and his utter hatred of his father fuels him. He raises the rifle and shoulders it in one motion, then fires without hesitation.

The doe staggers, a spray of dark exploding from its shoulder. George's ears ring from the shot, but he hears a whistling, then a squealing bleat. The worst thing he has ever heard. He rises to sprint after the doe, but his father grabs his arm in a vice grip from behind..

"Lemme go!" His voice is a squeal now. "I gotta save her!"

George twists free, and in one swift motion spins back to elbow his father square in the Adam's apple, right where he had aimed. His father grabs his neck, opens his mouth, but can only gurgle. George spits into his father's face, then sprints toward the sound of the dying deer.

PART FIVE
A SINGLE THING IN NATURE

"When one tugs at a single thing in nature, he finds it attached to the rest of the world."

— John Muir

NO SOCKS

Every morning Peter wakes at five, out of habit from his military days. It gets pretty noisy on the streets by that time anyway, and he knows he's unable to sleep much longer after that, even if he wanted to. But he doesn't really want to. He wants to be active and contributing. He wants to be wanted. He wants respect more than anything else. Something he's not felt since he lost his job, since he became unable to make both the rent and the utility bill, then just the rent. Since he started sleeping in his car, and after that got repossessed, on friends' couches. Then after all of the welcomes wore out, in the shelters, the parks, the loading docks.

On his second night on the streets of L.A., someone manages to take his duffle bag from under his head while he is sleeping. The following day he is beaten up for his jacket in broad daylight while walking through Elysian Park. Back when he had his car to sleep in, back when he was still in the suburbs of Orange County, he could keep pretty clean and truly believed he would land another job, but the poor economy causes his layoff, and the same poor economy means no other jobs anywhere else either. Peter meticulously keeps his clothes in good shape, despite the wrinkles and lack of laundering by wiping them down with wet paper towels each day when he takes a sponge bath in a public bathroom. For several months his clean appearance helps him to eat pretty well. It's easy to get a free meal at a pizza parlor because there are no table assignments or staff serving on the floor. All Peter has to do is grab a leftover silver tray and park himself in a booth, then watch the games on the giant TV while he keeps an eye out for people getting ready to leave, then nab their trays if there are any slices of 'za left. Amazing how much food people leave behind. Big, busy pizza parlors are the best. A lot of food everywhere and easy to blend in. No one pays attention, and if someone notices him grabbing a tray, he acts like he's just bussing the table and carries it to the front or to another room. Peter quickly discovers that softball teams sometimes leave nearly whole pizzas behind, especially if they are all drinking. Kids always seemed to leave leftover crusts, and adults will walk away with several inches of beer in their glasses. Weekends are the best because there's a constant flow of teams throughout the day, and that means easy food starting in the late mornings, and often one-more-for-the-road pitchers of beer ordered but only half poured. Sometimes there are baskets of wings, too. In the first few months in the shelters he can always get enough food for dinner at pizza parlors, and on the weekend, lunches too.

In Irvine, when the co-ed team of newspaper reporters wins the tournament and carries in a large plastic bag of championship t-shirts, they leave behind not just an extra shirt, but a North Face windbreaker with a wallet in the pocket. Peter has no problem taking food and drink that he knows will be tossed out anyway, but the wallet keeps him up for nights. Not the wallet itself, but the cash and credit cards. Because it happens right as he feels himself slipping, going to dark places in his head while trying to fall asleep. More and more he is unable to blend in, people reacting to his beard or smelly armpits. His car was repoed months ago. He is down to nothing, and things are only going to get worse. In the past week he has begun waking up confused and scared, and that scares him because he's never been afraid before in his life. The pain from his hunger actually wakes him up. He starts talking to his gramps in order to fall back asleep, but the cold is bothering his sore shoulder every time he lies down now, no matter what position, and even though he is less cold now that he has the team windbreaker, the wallet and cash are keeping him awake.

The address on the driver's license leads Peter to an ugly gated community. He studied design and architecture and these homes have no character. No soul. Huge McMansions with vinyl window casings and louvered blinds, designed to look Tuscan or Spanish or whatever the hell it was they were going for, all derivative and tasteless. Made for people who like pre-packaged ocean cruises and distance themselves from the common folk who don't have wealth. A guard gate to keep people like Peter out. The guard is ex-military, like him, he can tell by the spit-shine, the way he addresses him as he approaches and asks him his business. Peter doesn't want to mention the wallet because the guard will think he stole it and then detain him, so he says he's a gardener.

"A gardener, sir? Without a truck?"

He is denied access. Peter tells him the street address, which he has memorized, and also the cross street, which he learned from looking it up in a Thomas Guide in Sears. The guard tells him to move along or he will have to call the police for trespassing. When Peter looks back, the guard is taking Polaroid photos in his direction. When he looks back again, the guard is writing in his book.

Peter finds another way into the tract by hiking through the Thomas F. Riley Wilderness Park on the other side, which he also looked up in the Thomas Guide, and on the third try he finally manages to scale a wall where nothing but bulldozers are on the other side, ready to grade the hills for new streets and house foundations.

He leaves the wallet containing all of the credit cards and driver's license in the mailbox, along with a note apologizing for keeping the cash, for now, with an IOU promising to pay it all back as soon as he lands a job. He signs it with his first and middle names, "Peter Malcolm," so it will look like a full signature but so it will be impossible to trace him. He's going to pay it back anyway so it won't matter, he says to his gramps as he starts to spend the cash at last.

Two months later Peter is out of money and sleeping at the Midnight Mission in downtown Los Angeles, having been introduced to painkillers by a thin woman who had noticed the scrapes on his forearm from scaling the wall. She was sitting on the curb at the Fullerton train depot on Harbor Boulevard, and he believed her when she said she used to be a model but that the drugs had made her teeth go bad. She had offered him a blowjob for his windbreaker. He declined, but shared the half sandwich he had wrapped in a napkin in his pocket, left behind at a table at Denny's when he walked in to use the restroom. They hung out for three weeks until she started screaming at him, and when she clawed at his cheeks with her nails one morning, he hopped onto a rush hour commuter train and ended up at Union Station.

§

Peter is glad he has the windbreaker. The streets are a lot colder in LA for some reason. Maybe it's because there's more concrete, he thinks. That, and the winds whipping between the buildings, channeling tunnels of cold gusts.

He first meets Ramon at the Midnight Mission. He's a short ex-vet with eyes like a lamb and a moral code that he isn't afraid to share, which Peter likes. Especially now that he's having a hard time remembering exactly where he is when he wakes up, and the nightmares of 'Nam are coming more and more. When Ramon is around, Peter is calmer. Maybe because they keep to a routine. They do their sit-ups and push-ups together first thing in the morning, right after waking, just like in the Army, then walk down the "Head of the Nickel," as Ramon calls 5th Street, to the library where they wait for the doors to open. They take sponge baths in a basement bathroom and have a morning bowel movement before walking up the steps and greeting the librarian at the desk, then sitting down at a large table to read the morning newspapers, sharing sections. Peter finishes each morning library visit with the *New York Times* crossword puzzle, which he completes using one of the short yellow pencils from the small cardboard trays that sit on top of the card catalogs.

§

Peter is awakened by a hard sideways jolt. In his half-dream he's back in 'Nam and someone jumps on his back and hooks his arms behind him and presses his head forward in a full-nelson. He can hear the bullets whizzing past his ears but he can't lift his head and he can't get up. Then another jolt and he's in high school, his cheek pressed to the mat, about to be pinned in the CIF Championships, his coach yelling "Earthquake!" and when he looks over to him he opens his eyes and he's in the Midnight Mission and someone behind him is shouting "Earthquake! Run!" and the floor is rolling and he falls off the cot, hard. He looks around for Ramon, but he's gone, and a large piece of plaster drops next to his leg with a thud. Peter scrambles to his feet and runs out the door just as the ceiling comes crashing down behind him. He's standing on the street with a crowd that overflows the sidewalk. Shopkeepers up and down the block are inspecting their storefronts for damage, and there's shattered glass everywhere. Peter decides to walk a different route to the library, to check things out. At a storefront window painted "Steel's Café," the smell of bacon slows Peter's step and sets his stomach to whine. The aroma wafts through the frosted louvered windows above the front door. Must be a special place if the front window didn't shatter, Peter thinks. Then he realizes that the Midnight Mission probably isn't going to be able to feed anyone that day, and maybe not for a while, what with all the damage. So, maybe he could do a quick and clean dine-and-dash here.

Peter hates lying. His gramps made him promise never to do it, but he had resorted to making up fibs to his friends to explain why he had no money. After a couple of tales of being robbed, though, he had to finally admit to people that had been laid off, but even then he still hid the truth of his "living situation," and he would start inventing stories about places he had applied for work, and pretty soon, without even realizing it, the lies turned from temporary necessities to ways of keeping his dignity. He had gotten pretty good at it, too. So his plan now was to walk in and order steak and eggs, say he's waiting for someone but that he'll order first, then eat slow and casual-like, maybe read the paper if he sees one, take his time and act as if he's looking for his friend outside so the check wouldn't come too soon, then bolt out the front door when the waitress goes into the kitchen. Then never look back.

A metal strip sticking up beyond the top of the door tips a cow bell as he steps in, and he jumps from nerves and the unexpected loudness so close to his head.

—the hell?

No one is there though. Good. The regular customers must be dealing with the earthquake, Peter thinks. He slides into the first booth by the door and looks around. Every booth and table has a place setting, and everything looks pretty clean excepts for a large tub of dirty dishes at the far end of the counter.

Peter picks up a battered menu propped between the silver napkin holder and the window. He scans it quickly so he can say what he wants without hesitation whenever the waitress comes out. *"Good Morning Steak and Eggs: $2.50."* That sounds— A glass of water clunks onto the table and Peter jumps a bit. A man is standing beside the booth, wiping wet hands on his thick white apron. He is absolutely massive. *Oh boy. Not good.* Peter looks quickly back at the menu. A line drawing of a rooster on a fence, silhouetted in a circle of sun, with two half-notes floating out of its beak. *—What key?* The rooster blurs. He wonders if the man can hear his heart pounding. He's all shaky from the hunger. Say something quick.

"Ready to order?" The man beats him to it.

"Yeah, but uh, there's two of us."

"Two?"

"Yeah, he's—he's on his way. We'll need another water."

The waiter nods and disappears through swinging half-doors into the back. The stillness of the man's head as he walks makes him appear to glide, like a dancer, despite a massive six-foot six-inch frame and muscles like a wrestler. Peter hears the crunch of crushed ice being scooped, then the call of water as it rises in the glass. He thinks of his gramps, and how his word was his bond, and now his gaze shoots to the door as he considers running out before he has to lie again. Not too late. But his hunger holds him fast. It's been days. Gramps would understand.

The waiter returns with a dripping glass of ice water and sets it down next to the first.

Clunk.

Now what?

"So, you wanna order something to start with, or wait for your friend?"

Friend? For the first time Peter looks directly up at the man. He looks a bit like John Wayne, except he's black, and his hair is thin and short, salt and pepper. The man lifts his eyebrows, waiting for a reply.

Uh-oh, he's eyeing your clothes. He knows you have no money. Tell him Ramon's on his way.

"Um, Ramon is—"

No, he might make you wait. Order something quick before he gets suspicious.

"Nah, I think I'll go ahead..." Peter clears his throat and looks the man in the eye as if to prove he has nothing to hide. "I'm pretty hungry. I'll go ahead and order."

"Sure. What'll it be?"

Peter freezes. *What was it called again? The crowing rooster. Two notes...*

The waiter looks Peter up and down, stopping his eyes on his dirty bare ankles. Peter snatches his legs back in, banging his heels against the booth's pedestal. "I'm a gardener," Peter blurts instead of cursing at the pain. "I never wear socks."

The man looks at Peter squarely. "A gardener..."

"Yeah, socks collect dirt and foxtail burrs. I never wear 'em. I just cut two lawns early this morning, up in—" Before he can finish the lie, Peter's stomach lets out a moan, rising in pitch at the end like a question.

"You *do* have money, don't you friend?"

Shit. Peter squeezes his eyes shut. *Now what?*

The man eases down into the other side of the booth and puts his massive forearms on the table. "When's the last time you ate, son?"

Peter's pride wants to tell him that it was none of his business, but instead he opens his eyes and stares at the glasses of water in silence. The waiter sighs. *Do the right thing, Peter*, gramps says to him.

"I'm sorry," Peter says.

The waiter nods.

Okay, time to leave. His stomach growls again. "Sorry." He starts to slide out of the booth.

"Okay, look," the waiter says tapping on the window with the knuckle of his bent index finger. "See that? That says 'Steele's' right there".

Backwards.

"That's my name on the place. I'm Joseph Steele. I own this café."

"I said I was sorry."

Joseph leans across the table. "Right, so my dishwasher's been out sick all week, and no one is here this morning because of the earthquake, and I've got three tubs of dirty dishes from yesterday sitting in the kitchen with no one to wash 'em" He jerks his thumb toward the back. "Now, I'm gonna need some clean plates for the lunch crowd when they come." Then his voice softens. "If they come. Look, tell you what. How 'bout you go wash them for me, and when you get done, I'll fix you some steak and eggs."

Good Morning Steak and Eggs! Two notes. Peter nods and starts to slide out of the booth. Then he stops and juts his chin. "And some coffee."

Joseph shakes his head, amused. "All right, and some coffee."

"And some juice."

"Don't push it."

Peter stops and looks down to the menu. The rooster on the fence comes back into focus. He is flooded with butterflies. *Food is on the way. Hallelujah.*

"What the hell," Joseph says, sliding out of the booth and rapping his knuckles twice on the table, "I might even cook you up some home style potatoes if you do a good job."

What kind of man is this? And what does he want in return? Lying, dishonest Peter. About to steal from him! What a bastard. How could I even look him in the eye, much less sit in his restaurant, accept his free food? Peter thinks of his gramps again. *You can't even bring yourself to thank him?* Peter stares at the two glasses of water, his focus blurred on infinity, and make a solemn vow to himself that he will never lie to this man, Joseph Steele, again.

Joseph stands and stuffs the order pad into his back pocket. "Deal?"

"Deal," Peter answers, without looking up. "But I gotta be out of here by ten thirty. I got three more lawns to cut today."

Peter is annoyed when he sees all the dishes he has to wash. The dirty plates, saucers, and cups rise well beyond the walls of the three plastic tubs.

Joseph reaches in front of him and turned on the taps. "You want an apron?"

Peter shakes his head. Joseph hands him a brush and a sponge.

"This is more like six tubs."

Joseph grins. "You're a work of art, son."

"Yeah?"

"Yeah. And for some reason, I like you."

"Then crack me a couple extra eggs, maybe, if you like me so much."

Joseph pats him on the back. "I'll get that fourth tub from up front. Then we'll see about that." Then he adds, "But you'll have to do a good job."

Peter thinks some of the dishes must have been sitting for days. Sure enough, the food is caked on hard when he starts to wash them. Yellow-orange egg yolk webbed between fork tines is the toughest, but when he holds it under a pelting stream of hot water it gives way. He loses his frustration as he loses track of time, and in the soothing meditation of repetition he is surprised when he reaches for more dishes but all of the tubs are empty. To his left, on the counter, the mountains from the tubs have been reordered into rows of like shapes and colors, all neatly filed and dripping in long racks. Peter notices there are two different sizes of forks, and that there are more tall forks in the back bin, so he moves all of the short forks to the front and all of the tall ones to the back. Good. Then he notices that one of the deeper saucers has somehow found its way in among the thinner ones, but there are no more slots left in the rack, so Peter pulls one of the big plates from the rack and shuffles the others down to make room for one more. The rack looks perfect now with everything in its place, balanced and ordered, like a Bauhaus building Peter thinks, and he is pleased until he remembers the one extra dinner plate he's been holding in his hand for who knows how long and he doesn't want to disappoint Joseph by messing up the harmony of the rack.

—unfair.

Peter stands there, holding the plate. His hand aches. He switches it to the opposite hand. He forgets what he's doing. He looks around. Then he bends down and opens the cabinet underneath the sink. He slides the plate between a tall bottle of soap and a jug of cleaning solution. *Good deal.* No one will be able to tell that anything is out of place once he shuts the doors.

The next thing he knows he's dragging his fork in circles through his eggs. *I wondered if my mom knew how to scramble eggs. Wait. Did she scramble these?* Peter looks up, but he is alone. How long has he been there? The sharp taste of steak blood makes him remember. *Good Morning Steak and Eggs. Two notes.*

"Hey?"

The thinness of his voice rings across the room and fades.

Weird.

Joseph walks through the swinging doors from the kitchen.

Oh. Right.

"You finally done?" Joseph asks.

Peter gets a wave of sadness. "No."

Joseph pours himself a cup of coffee, and starts to whistle softly. Peter notices that the red towel tucked into Joseph's waist matches the red of the cigarette machine. And above the machine on the wall is a small brown photograph in a red frame. *Red. Red. Red.*

"What's that?" Peter asks, leaning to look around Joseph.

"What? The photo?" Joseph gestures to the picture with his cup.

"That's Angels Flight."

Angels Flight!

Peter clanks his cup down hard and slides quickly out of the booth. He walks to the photo and tries to put his face close to it, but the cigarette machine is in the way.

"They just tore her down two years ago, you know..." Joseph says he remembers sitting on the adjacent hillside and watching the men in the white masks disconnect the cars from the cable, that it reminded him of the doctors who had unplugged his wife's life support after she passed. Same week, too. Joseph closed the café and sat and watched all day as they hooked the cars to a crane and swung them onto the back of a flat-bed truck, one at a time, then rolled them away. "Just like that. Gone."

"My gramps took me to Angels Flight for my birthday one year and gave me an Etch-a-Sketch," Peter says.

"No kiddin'? My grandparents used to take me to ride on her too. You may not believe this, but Grandpa Steele was the one who helped design Angels Flight, back in the day."

Peter turns and looks at up at him, but Joseph keeps his eyes on the photo. "Course, they changed the design of the cars and track later, and grandpa never got credit for it because of— well, because colored folk in those days... People called us a lot worse, you can believe that now. But yes, Grandpa Steele designed the first cars. And the tracks." He taps the glass with his fingernail. "The original cars looked a lot different than these, though."

Peter taps the glass too. "The barber shop on Sixth has a pic of Angels Flight where the track bends up steeper. I've only seen it through the window though. Every time I walk by, the shop's closed." Peter doesn't mention how he had run out of the shop after his haircut and never gone back. Peter steps closer until his toes are against the cigarette machine, and he bends his upper torso toward the photo.

It's a sepia tone, taken sometime in the early twenties. Peter remembers the photo from when he studied architecture at U.S.C. The photographer is standing on Second Street, looking west toward Bunker Hill. In the center of the frame is the dark half circle of the Third Street tunnel. To the left of that, between the tunnel and the drug store, stands the shrine-like vault at the foot of Angels Flight. A child stands at the gate, holding the hand of a man in a hat. Their backs are turned away and they are looking uphill, waiting for one of the cars to descend.

"My gramps' hands were rough on the inside, but the backs were soft," Peter says. "His skin got thin and speckled." Peter remembers the heat of his hand inside his grandfather's.

"You ever hear about Colonel Eddy? The man who built Angels Flight?" Peter hears Joseph's voice floating from behind him. "J.W. Eddy. Everyone called him Colonel. He was good friends with my grandma and grandpa both. Fact, he was best man at their wedding."

The sun slants warm on Peter's face through the front windows.

"Grandma used to say if it wasn't for the Colonel, I might never have been born."

Joseph jerks his head toward the booth and begins walking toward it. Peter follows, looking at the dust motes dancing in slow motion across the white wedge of light that falls across the table.

This is nice.

"Let's see now," Joseph slides into the booth. "Grandpa first met the Colonel, oh, back in the mid-1890s, it must have been. The Colonel had just moved from here from Arizona. He and Grandpa worked together on the Kern River Project for the L.A. Electric Power Company, bringing electricity from the north down to Los Angeles."

"My dad dug ditches too."

"That right? Huh. Well, my grandpa was an excellent builder, and Eddy, being a civil engineer, took a liking to him. Actually, the Colonel started out as a school teacher, my grandpa told me. Then he studied law, I think he said. Anyway, got himself elected as State Representative from Indiana. No, wait. Illinois I think it was. Wherever it was, I know he eventually became State Senator somewhere. Wound up being real close friends with Abe Lincoln, of all people. Led the campaign to get him elected." He cut off a piece of steak and popped it into his mouth.

Where did that steak come from?

"Imagine that. People have no perspective of time when it comes to anything that came before they were born. But it wasn't that long ago, really, if you think about it. I mean, there are people alive right now who were slaves when they were kids." Joseph shakes his head and slurps some coffee. "Just saw one interviewed on the Today Show. The world's changed a lot in the last hundred years. Airplanes. The electric light..." Joseph points to the ceiling with his knife and looks back down at his steak and cuts off another piece as he chews.

Peter looks at Joseph's arms, and for the first time notices ashy, lighter splotches.

"Back then, Bunker Hill was where all the rich folks lived, not like it is now. You ever seen photos of the mansions? Remarkable. Mom said they used to call Bunker Hill 'The Jewel in the Crown' since all the homes were so bright. Real ornate like. All the cut glass windows. Anyway, the old Bradbury Mansion over on Court and Hill was my favorite. Grandma loved the Crocker Home best. Some people said ships at sea could see the Crocker shining from way offshore." Joseph smiles and shakes his head. "I don't know about that."

"Maybe because the sun reflects off the windows," Peter says.

Joseph looks up at Peter, who is staring at the photo on the wall. "Why, I never thought of that. But that might be it. Huh. Makes sense. You know, I remember in the Navy, even in the daylight we could see blinkers flashing Morse code from ships forty, fifty miles away." Joseph nods. "May be. Yeah."

Joseph gestures with his fork. "Kinda funny you should say that 'cause it was my dad who dreamed the specific design of the cars, and he's the one who made the windows those odd shapes because of the grade of the hill it rode on. I wonder if he got it from the beveled mansion windows. Huh."

"I wouldn't know," Peter says.

Joseph chuckles. "No, you wouldn't. Anyway, you gotta remember, Bunker Hill was a lot steeper back then. There was no way to get to the top without going around, those days. So the Colonel petitioned city council for a franchise. You know politicians. If there's a straight point between two lines you can be sure they'll find a way to make it zig and zag. Sure as hell, somebody on the council convinces all the others that Eddy might have a monopoly if his railcars are the only access to the top of the hill. So they end up making a provision that he has to build a stairway alongside the Flight, so that anyone can get to the top for free without riding if they want to. My grandpa always said the Colonel was a pretty good talker, and I guess that was true 'cause he gave the City his word and they granted him a permit right there. And Colonel kept his promise, too. Paid for it all out of his own pocket."

Joseph pauses and squints out of the window to the street.

"I'd go every day after school and play on those steps. I used to pretend I'd be climbing up the side of a pyramid in Egypt, or in the Foreign Legion storming some fort up on top of a dune. Yes sir... And when I was a cop, I found a body on those steps one night. Young woman. A knife in the back of her neck."

"You were a cop?" Peter asks.

"Thirty years. Medal of Valor."

Peter thinks of the plate he hid in the cabinet under the sink.

He starts to feel nauseated. Joseph takes a sip of coffee.

"Now when Eddy got the permit to build her, my grandpa was, oh, twenty-six, twenty-seven. About that. He was already best friends with the Colonel by now, having worked as his assistant on the Kern project and all, and so the Colonel called him up and hired him as 'co-designer and chief engineer.' Imagine that. One of the first negroes ever to be called Chief Engineer. But grandpa said it was almost as if he was given some kind of magical vision or something because the very night that Eddy hired him, the design for Angels Flight appeared to grandpa in a dream. He woke up, sketched it all out, and went back to bed. Boom. Before you know it, there she was, rising up Bunker Hill."

Like a dream. Peter remembers the face of his gramps smiling down, the rough hand holding his as they walked those same steps. How his hand sweated in his grip. Then Peter imagines a woman with a knife in the back of her neck, with Joseph bending down over her, picking her up in his arms, carrying her down to Hill Street like a limp child. *Pieta.*

"The dedication ceremony was where my grandpa and grandma first met," Joseph says. He stares through the window out into the street now, his eyes sparkling. "The Colonel planned the grand opening for New Year's Eve. 1901. He even took out a big ad in the Times inviting everyone down for a free ride. He was such a showman, you know." Joseph grins. "Grandpa said everybody knew all about it anyway so he was wasting his money. But Colonel liked a spectacle. It had been the talk of the town since they first broke ground, of course. Sure enough, people came all the way from Bakersfield and San Diego to see her launch. Now my grandmother, bless her soul, she was only fifteen years old at the time, and I guess her mother was a leading member of a social group known as 'The Ladies of Olive Heights'—that's what they called that section of Bunker Hill back then, Olive Heights. Well, the way grandpa tells it, the Colonel introduces grandma's mom to him and grandpa says hello and..." Joseph pauses and looks back to his plate. "Then he takes one look at my grandmother standing there in her blue dress with her pretty eyes and bang—he falls in love with her right then. Quick as you can say Red Car Railroad."

Red Car Railroad.

"Well, the Colonel pulls grandpa away so they can stand at the very front of the first car to run that day, and that impresses grandma and her mom quite a bit, doncha know. He was pretty light skinned, or else there might have been a riot." Joseph chuckles and looks at Peter. "I guess there were so many people who showed up early to ride, that the Mayor, who had insisted that he be the first *official* passenger, doesn't even get to ride until the fifth or sixth carload. Anyway, my grandpa and the Colonel are standing on the back end of the first car, waving to the crowd, and they start rising up to Olive Street Station to *oohs* and *aahs*, but instead of looking out over the city and the beautiful skyline, grandpa can't take his eyes off my grandma. He just stands there staring at her face all the way to the top and all the way back down."

Way back...

"Back at the bottom, the Colonel makes a speech to the crowd that was spilling out onto Hill Street by this point, proclaiming that every man, woman and child rides for free that day. Of course, everybody cheers! So all day long, as soon as a person would step off, they'd get back in line and ride again. Well, the Colonel finishes his speech by pointing out that, even though the rides are free that day, there just so happens to be a coin box in the plaza, just in case anyone is so inclined to make a contribution! That Colonel..."

Joseph smiles and shakes his head. Peter stares across the room at the photo.

"Now, grandpa's standing right beside the Colonel as he's

making his speech and he still can't take his eyes off of grandma. And grandma's so shy. You know, blushing. All the while the Colonel has been curling his white handlebar mustache with his fingers as he talks, and with a flash in his eye he points out that the slot in the top of the contribution box is just the perfect size for a twenty dollar gold piece! The crowd roars and applauds, and the Colonel elbows my grandpa to punctuate the joke, but grandpa's lost in a dream staring at grandma. He jumps startled-like and the crowd roars again. A few people up front start whispering back and forth, nodding. And that makes grandma blush even more..."

Joseph gazes out the window, his eyes sparkling. "So, the constable closes down Hill Street from carriage traffic and everybody is swarming at the gates to either get in line and ride or talk to the Colonel and shake his hand and thank him, and eventually grandpa makes his way back to the table where grandma is serving punch. He introduces himself again and asks her if she'll grant him the honor of riding with her on the Flight. Grandma turns to ask her mom and she nods yes, and even nudges her forward, the way she told it. Knowing grandpa was so close to the Colonel and all, well, she was probably proud as she could be. Grandma grabs her dress and steps from behind the table, and grandpa offers her his arm and she giggles a bit. She told me it was the first time she ever took a man's arm, and that she never took anyone else's her whole life. So grandpa leads her up to the hoop gates where the Colonel waves them past the crowd to climb aboard, and grandpa takes her hand to help her on..."

...*to help...*

"Grandma says they rode up and down, up and down, all afternoon, not getting off, just riding on the back of an Angel. I guess right about dusk they got off at the top and sat there at Angels Rest to watch the sun set into the Pacific out on the horizon. Grandma says she fell in love that very day and decided that grandpa would be the man she would marry. Of course, grandpa says he had already decided that the first time he looked into her eyes..."

Joseph's voice trails off. Peter's eyes are shut. Peter waits for him to continue, but all is silent.

"Oh!" Joseph says, breaking the mood.

Peter opens his eyes. Joseph is looking at his watch.

"It's almost eleven thirty. You'd better get moving if you still got all those lawns to cut."

Peter's neck prickles. He looks down at his plate. A last bite of steak. He sniffs and stabs it, then pulls it off the tines with his teeth. As he chews he tries to think of what to say, not enjoying anything half as much as before. He swallows. It hurts.

Peter slides out of the booth and looks at Joseph's hands spread on each side of his plate.

"Thanks for washing the—"

But Peter runs out the door just as an aftershock jolts the city again, the cowbell clanking behind him, car horns honking in front of him.

IN THE LAND OF DROUGHT

Harrison's halfway down to the water when he sees the rifle. Some kid a couple hundred yards away is swinging the barrel around, sighting things in the distance, aiming at a hawk circling above. "Boom!" Harrison can hear him say, the words skipping echo across the distance.

The two of them are in the white barren silt where the lake used to be. In this time of drought, the lake has receded down into the Earth, creating a kind of no man's land a quarter mile long filled with the ashy remains of what used to be underwater plants and fish.

To Harrison, the kid looks like his son, Stanley, but then every boy reminds him of Stanley lately. Stanley, who is in juvenile detention right now after breaking some poor kid's arm with a bat for striking out during baseball practice. Stanley, who is locked up because this is not his first offense, not even his fifth. Stanley, the sociopath Harrison has apparently raised to be a bully, whom Harrison loves as if he is still a five year old.

"Gareth," the kid in the once-lake yells up to his friend leaning against the hood of a car at the top of hill. When Gareth looks down at the kid, he holds the rifle above his head like it's a barbell and yells a long, "Woooo!"

For a moment, Harrison thinks the kid is celebrating a kill. That doesn't make sense though. He didn't hear a bang, and there are too many people up and down this unnaturally long beach. No one but Stanley would be reckless enough to hunt in a place like this.

Most of these people have stopped what they're doing to watch the kid celebrate whatever has happened. A man twenty yards off lets his metal detector droop and stares up at him with a sideways kind of smile.

"Do you think we should stop him?" the man with the metal detector asks.

The kid is laughing now, excited by his luck. He's drawing a bead on Gareth up the hill. "I don't know," Harrison says. "It can't be dangerous right? A gun down at the bottom of a lake like that." He hears his own words. Maybe his weakness has allowed his son to become a bully.

The man walks closer to Harrison. "If a shell had been left in there, it could have dried out by now, I suppose." The man cups his free hand to his mouth. "Be careful," he calls, but the kid is trotting up the hill and doesn't seem to notice.

Harrison should stop the boy, he knows, but whatever strength he had has been sapped out of him lately. Instead, he nods at the metal detector. "Find anything?"

"Some nails and hooks and things, and look at this." He holds a white lump of something out to Harrison.

Harrison holds it in his palm. It's carved soapstone, white with light blue streaks running through it, but the shape is hard to understand. Then he sees the rough outlines of what was once clearly a carved bear, eroded now a little, so the paws are smoothed out, the snout softening away.

"Where did you find this?"

The man points with the tip of his beard. "Over there across the lake. It's a good find, isn't it?"

"Good find, yeah," Harrison says. "It should be in a museum."

This last remark is just meant to be a compliment about what great eyes the man has, but he stiffens, and Harrison realizes that the man is considering his government uniform. He has to be thinking that Harrison is law enforcement, here to take something away. He isn't going to keep the bear, wouldn't know what to do with it if he did, and doubts that it's any kind of major find, but he can feel the heat in the man starting to rise, feel the argument about to begin.

Maybe he should argue, but instead before the man speaks, Harrison hands the carved bear back. He thinks he can see the future of this bear. It has been sitting here in the lake for who knows how many years, and now it will be just as lost sitting on this man's mantel. He'll be excited about it and then it will be as lost to humanity as it would have been down here, tossed into the trash by his heirs or broken in half by a little boy. Still, what else is there besides the clumsy loss of everything good in this ashy world of drought?

He's going to say something more to the man, but the young man's scream cuts him off: "I'm John fucking Wayne." He's grabbed the rifle by the barrel and is swinging it around and around his head. "I'm King fucking Kong."

"Stop," the man calls.

Harrison has a vision of what could happen, the rifle discharging, a hundred-year-old piece of shrapnel lodging itself in the kid's brain. He sees Stanley's stupid reckless bat as though he were there when he did it. He sees him beat that poor nerdy kid on the baseball field. "Stop," he yells. "Stop, Goddamn you."

The kid doesn't hear him. Gareth is clapping and laughing. The two of them have started to dance around. Maybe they're drunk, Harrison thinks. Maybe they're high.

"Stop it!" Harrison screams, but something about this world tamps his voice down. His words arc into the air but they're sucked back into this filthy white hole, this place that once shrouded the land with its water.

DAUGHTER OF THE MAMMOTH HUNTER

From the top of the hill, they look like dogs to her, so she jumps up and down between her parents and yells her word for dog again and again. She likes the way that when they step on the ground, she can hear them as long as there is no wind and the birds have gone to sleep. That night, they walk past the camp and wake her from her dreams. She holds her breath in the dark. She yells her favorite word into the moonlight wisps of fog: dog and dog and dog.

IN THE LAND OF BEARS

WHEN DARLENE sees the picture of her father hugging Prissy, she isn't sure what she is supposed to feel. Her mother tells her that Prissy is her father's first wife, who he married and who died in a car accident years before her parents met. Darlene decides by Christmas that she should feel sorry for her father, and by Valentine's Day, the woman takes on a mysterious air, and her father seems like a tragic figure who has lost a charming and sophisticated woman and tried to replace her with the conservative lump who is Darlene's mother. Now, he seems trapped in a life of bitter responsibility with a partner he doesn't love and three children. In the picture, Prissy is wearing the kind of jewelry her mother never does. She has a purple silk scarf and perfectly round, oversized sunglasses just like Audrey Hepburn in *Breakfast at Tiffany's*. She laughs with abandon at something, and her father watches Prissy with unveiled longing mixed with amusement for her carefree attitude. Yes, the proper point of view is that the loss of Prissy is the tragic and defining event of her father's life.

All of this she decides without talking to her father. She doesn't want to remind him of everything that he has lost when this woman in the pearl earrings left him. By Easter, she has constructed a fantasy life for her father where he was once dashing and carefree. He told Darlene once that he'd studied flying, and she thinks he would have been a pilot had if not for her mother. When Darlene hears him groan or sigh, she wonders if he is caught in the memory of that past and perfect life when everything was electric, and he was so perfect himself.

With Easter weekend, Spring break comes, and Shelly, her cousin on her father's side, invites Darlene up to the mountains to go skiing. Shelly lives up above 5,000 feet near Lake Arrowhead, and something about the location of her house, and her relation to her father makes that side of the family feel romantic and free. They are people who lived up away from the city. They seem unafraid, both of the bears that live near them and the treacherous drive. The roads ice over, but they drive on despite the nearness of cliffs that she can't even see over.

Besides the skiing, she wants to talk to her cousin, and maybe her aunt and uncle about Prissy. The first chance Darlene gets, when the two girls are totally alone on the ski lift, Darlene brings the subject up. She asks, "Did your parents ever tell you about Prissy, my father's first wife?"

Shelly's eyes narrow. Below her is a hundred feet of oxygen ending with the hard packed snow. Shelly never seems to mind the imminence of death, and now she frowns at Darlene and shakes her head. She says, "My father told me once that I'm not supposed to talk about Prissy, but I will if you want."

"Why not?"

She shrugs. "I don't think it's some big secret except Dad said some things you just don't talk about. I don't think I'm even supposed to know, but they caught me snooping one time, and they knew there was no avoiding it."

A hot tingling passes over Darlene's body. She forgets about the height nearly completely. "Who was she?"

"My dad and mom have pictures of her, and they told me some of the stories." Shelly tells her about the wedding, which was outside under some pine trees at a place near Shelly's house. She knows this because her parents kept the wedding pictures. Darlene asks about the dress and the decorations, and it's painful when the ski lift dumps them at the top of the run because she knows she'll have to wait until they are all the way down and back on the lift again before she'll be able to ask about her father's romantic, previous life.

That becomes the pattern of the day. On the lift, Darlene steers the conversations towards Prissy as much as she can. Shelly wants to talk about the friends she plans to introduce to Darlene, and she knows only so much about Prissy, but Darlene tries to squeeze everything she can out of the hints and photographs her cousin came across. On the way down the run, she mourns her father's lost life. She wonders what he was like then. He has become serious and single-minded, perhaps even closed off. Had he been exciting before? Shelly says that if Darlene wants to, they could try to sneak into her parent's bedroom and get ahold of the pictures. It might be dangerous, but it could be worth it too.

By three o'clock, Darlene is physically exhausted, but mentally more energized than she was when the day started, and when Shelly falls down on the slope and bruises her thigh badly, Darlene is almost thankful because she knows that will be the end of skiing for the two of them that day. As they change in the locker room, Shelly admits that she wanted to end early too because she'd gotten the two of them invitations to a get-together. A get-together, not a party, Darlene thinks. The word suggests something to her. It is the sort of thing that Prissy would have gone to. It's the kind of thing that they do up here in the mountains after a day of skiing. It suggests red wine and conversation with people who have seen the world.

Back at the cabin, Shelly disappears into her parents' bedroom for a moment and rushes back into her room before anyone can see what she is doing. Darlene follows her, and the two girls sit on Shelly's bed picking through pictures of Prissy and her father's wedding out of a shoe box full of snapshots. "They didn't want you to see these, but they'll never know."

Her father is thin in the pictures, and Darlene has never seen him like that. She is staring at his handsome alter ego without those permanent dark circles under his eyes, and the slumped shoulders that he's gotten from sixteen years of trying to provide for his children. The man before her is not the man she knows, and while Shelly goes into the bathroom to get ready, Darlene tries to get to know the man by the eyes in the photo. What kind of person was he? There is something about him that seems almost dangerous to her, in a sort of 1950s way. He had a flipped up collar and a smile that was nearly a sneer, but it wasn't danger, really, she decides. It is youth and life. It is impossible to know what her life would have been if Prissy had been her mother, but she knows that it would have been different because she could see that with Prissy, her father had been a different sort of man.

Eventually, Darlene lies down on Shelly's bed thinking about her father and creating a romantic dream about the way it must have been for him once. He had been one of these people up here. He had the same vitality and courage. She could see him driving on these mountain roads, along cliffs, when the blacktop was iced over, and the tires slipped at every curve. He must have been like Shelly's father who would laugh when the car would skid for a moment and make a joke or call out that it was good luck and good sense to lose your grip every once in a while. Now her father was living down the mountain in a single story ranch house that looked exactly like the one next to it and the one next to that one. What would she have been like if she had grown up here? Would her life have been filled with skiing and boys and girls like Shelly who thinks nothing of snooping in her parents' bedroom? Dreaming of this life, she allows the fatigue of the day catch up with her, and she drifts off to sleep on Shelly's bed.

Darlene wakes in the darkened room to Shelly caressing her face and telling her to wake up. "They're here," Shelly says.

Darlene blinks and looks around the room. She can't remember where she is. She knows she isn't in danger, but she's woken up from a dream and isn't even sure exactly who Shelly is. "Who's here?"

"My friends. I told you about them. They're here." Darlene

forces her consciousness up to the surface and understands who she is and what is happening. "Except the get-together's canceled. We're just going to hang out here."

"Here?"

"Yeah. My parents went out for the night, and none of us really wanted to go all the way down to Arrowbear anyway, which is where it is. The traffic's going to be terrible, so we're staying here, except, I need this room." That forces Darlene to her feet. She senses something in Shelly's voice, in the way that she says the word "need" that tells her this is going to be a special night for Shelly. Wobbling on her feet, she understands what kind of thing is going to happen, and it makes Darlene long for that other life, the one that she would have had if Prissy had been her mother, that bold sophisticated life where a girl wasn't kept in a state of protected childhood far longer than she had to be.

Darlene touches her hair. She says, "But I didn't have a chance to shower or anything."

Shelly waves a hand at her. "Are you kidding? You're better looking than the rest of us combined." Shelly gets behind her and pushes her out into the dazzling electric light of the kitchen where she blinks and squints, shading her eyes with the back of her left hand. There are people in here, and though she is wearing blue jeans and a sweatshirt, since she slept in her clothes, she feels as if she is wearing pajamas in front of strangers.

Someone, a boy, laughs at her. It isn't a mean laugh, just a laugh, and he says, "Good morning."

There is a group of four people sitting at a table, and she can't see them clearly, but she can tell at least that there are three males and a female. A feminine voice says, "Ah, too bad for Troy. She's much too young for you."

"Maybe."

The world sorts itself out for Darlene, and soon she can see who is there. Shelly comes up behind her and grabs one of the boys by the hand, dragging him back into the room with her, closing the door behind them, and as Darlene's eyes begin to adjust to the light, she can see what she is up against. She hasn't seen Shelly's boyfriend clearly and thinks of him as just a dark-haired blur, but what is left are a woman and two men. Men and a woman, not boys and a girl. They are smiling at her, and Darlene's eyes gravitate to the safety of the feminine face first. She is what Darlene has always thought of as a mountain woman, in blue jeans and a pink t-shirt peeping out from behind a big leather jacket. A curling stream of smoke rises off her cigarette, and a bottle of beer sit before her. The woman introduces herself as Colleen before taking a drag from her cigarette.

Colleen's boyfriend is named H. No name apparently, just H. They're adults, probably college age although there are no colleges up here. She had heard that Shelly hung with people who are older than she is. Here they are before her, and there is something shocking about them. When they hear Shelly giggle from her bedroom door, the three of them smile to each other and move out of the kitchen. As they go into the living room, Darlene casts furtive glances at the man she was supposed to be set up with. He's Troy, bigger than her father and muscular too. Probably a football player in high school, she thinks, and he probably still works out. He has a short, blond crew cut, and walking behind him, she can smell the beer and cigarettes he's finished. It isn't a bad smell. In fact, it's masculine.

In the living room, H sits on the wing chair with Colleen on his lap. Troy sits on the couch with plenty of room for Darlene, but she plops down cross-legged on the floor with her back to the fireplace. While she's been dozing, someone lit a fire there that will be dying soon if no one stokes it, and it makes her wonder how long she's been out. She reaches up to smooth her hair, but Colleen waves a dismissive hand at her. She says, "You look fine. You're great." And the men smile. Troy's eyes are on her for a moment but glance shyly away. It isn't what she would have expected from a guy who looks like him, and she relaxes a little.

H says, "So you and Shelly went skiing today." Darlene nods. "Was it terrible?"

She frowns. "Why would it be terrible?"

Colleen smiles. "He didn't mean anything. It's just that we all know what a bad skier she is."

"Oh well. I live down in the valley, and I barely get a chance to go skiing at all, so she's better than I am."

"God, you must have been falling all day," Colleen says, but she says it with a friendly smile that doesn't seem snide.

"It's just wonderful being up here." It was wonderful. That long conversation, and the dream-like state she's been in since she's come. She fell on the slope a few times, but she's used to that. It always seems a part of skiing.

Colleen leans her head back and looks at the ceiling. "I'm trying to remember the last time I went skiing."

H pokes her stomach. "That time we rented a place over in Big Bear."

She makes a face at him and laughs. "No," she said. "That was the last time *we* went skiing. There's a difference." She smiles secretively, and Darlene knows there's a joke there that brings them together. It's love, romance really, the kind that she's always wanted. Maybe she's still half asleep, but she knows that this was what Prissy and her father had been like together. It might even be that her father had been like Shelly and her boyfriend who make themselves known every once in a while with an indistinguishable sound or a laugh. He could have been anyone, but it seems obvious that he wasn't the same man he is today.

Colleen shakes off the private moment and starts talking about the last skiing trip she and H took, the one to Big Bear, and Darlene leans back and listens. The fire warms her back and goes into her bones, and though she hears the words Colleen is saying, the story washes over her, comforting her. She should have a glass of wine. That would warm her too, but somehow she just can't go into her uncle's pantry to get one. It's enough to be here and let the conversation grow between these three friends. In fact, it's enough just to be in the room, and she would prefer to be ignored. As a child, she would often fall asleep on the rug listening to the grown-ups talk, lulled by the rhythm of their chatter, and she wishes that she could do that now, but she can't, so she asks questions every once in a while just for appearances.

Eventually, the conversation softens and dies, and the four of them are lost in their own thoughts. Outside it has grown foggy and dark, but inside, the light of the one bulb burning in the room gives them a circle of comfort and warmth. H breaks the spell by saying to Colleen, "You want to..." He finishes the statement with his eyes which dart to a back bedroom.

As a response, Colleen smiles wickedly, and they rise slowly saying goodnight for now to Troy and Darlene. Troy just nods, and they disappear. When they are gone, Troy smiles at Darlene, and she smiles back. Throughout the night, they have not spoken to each other. It has been a part of the pattern. They have been in the same conversation but have directed their comments to H and Colleen. Now, Darlene climbs into the chair the couple abandoned, and the two of them watch the fire. In a moment, they can hear the radio click on in a back bedroom. Some country song that Darlene has never heard comes on. She strains to hear the lyrics, but they stay just out of reach. Finally, Troy says, "It's awkward, I know, but you have to forgive them."

"There's no need."

But he keeps going as though she's said nothing. "They never get to be alone."

"What, do they have children?"

"Children?" His eyebrows rise in surprise. "No, they both still live with their parents."

"Oh." The thought is strange to her. They seem so grown up and sophisticated, but maybe things are different up here.

"You don't have to worry about me," Troy says. "You're too young for me." He watches her as though he is checking to see if her feelings are hurt, but she isn't hurt. She's too young for him, and he's too old for her.

They slip back into quiet, the sound of the fire and distant music filling the room only broken occasionally by a knocking sound or a voice whose meaning could be interpreted any way they want to. In a while, Troy stands and goes into the kitchen. She can hear him going into the refrigerator and getting another bottle of beer. The refrigerator door closes, and the bottle is placed on the counter, but then silence. In a moment, his voice comes out of the kitchen in an excited whisper. "Darlene," he says in a way that makes her rise and go to him.

In the kitchen, he points out the window. She stands next to him, pressing her body against his so she can see what he is pointing out. In the backyard, a mass moves through the fog. She stares at it a moment. It's on all fours, but she can't understand what it is exactly. She asks Troy what she's looking at.

"It's a bear."

The bear's features seem to work themselves out—the great head, the hunched back, and if she squints, she can see the front legs. "I thought they were supposed to hibernate in the winter."

He shrugs. "I did too. I don't know what would wake her up. Maybe the winter's not cold enough."

The bear is looking for something, but Darlene can't think what it might be at first. It scratches at some mound under the snow and brings up something that glints. Darlene squints. "Beer bottles," she says. The bear licks them gently, caressing them with its tongue as if they are newborn cubs until either it has gotten all the nutrition it can out of them or it is bored with trying. It lifts its head and turns to the window. Darlene can't see the bear's eyes, but she knows the bear is looking directly at her, judging her. She feels that she should smile or wave, but she just stands there maintaining even eye contact with this great woman on the mountain. Eventually, the bear turns away and drifts off into the fog like some giant, silent iceberg in the Atlantic, and Darlene and Troy stand squinting at where it was hoping that they will see it again, but it never comes back. They turn to each other and smile, and Darlene realizes that she's been pressed up against him this whole time. Behind her, she hears Shelly moan in what is unmistakably sexual climax, and she can feel herself blush.

"Pretty good," he says.

"Yeah." He begins to move away, but she grabs him by the front of his jacket and holds him there. "I know I'm too young for you, but I want to kiss you."

He stares at her a moment with a bemused look on his face. He laughs quietly at something only he understands. "All right," he says, and he leans forward kissing her deeply but with his lips closed. From what her friends said, a boy needs to open his mouth to do a grown-up kiss, but his lips are closed, and she doesn't feel his tongue, and it is still passionate. She presses her body against his, and when it is done, he pushes her gently away and chuckles to himself. A moan comes out of the back bedroom, and Troy stops to listen to it for a second as though he could gather information from it the way that an animal gathers information from birdsong. He shakes his head, grabs his beer, and goes into the living room.

Darlene gazes into the backyard where the bear has gone and wishes that it would come back, and on an impulse, she opens the back door and walks over to where it had been. The snow bites her bare feet, but it's all right. When she is across the yard, she stands on her tiptoes as though that extra bit of height will make it easier to see through the dark wall of fog. At her feet, the prints lead away. She sticks her reddening left foot where the bear's paw was and smiles to see it engulfed.

"Darlene?" Troy is at the back door. The beer is in his hand, and he leans up against the door frame like he's James Dean or something. "What are you doing?"

Darlene laughs to see him there. Troy holds out his hand.

"Come back in here you little idiot," but he says it with a smile in his voice. "You don't know what's out there." It's true, so her stomach clenches in excitement, and she begins to take a step toward him. She thinks about what they are going to do after she walks across the snow and takes his hand, but at the sound of something crashing through the underbrush behind her, she spins on the ball of her foot, and that makes her laugh too. As she laughs, she imagines that her voice is powerful enough at that moment to echo through the woods like a gunshot or the moan of an animal. It will go past that great bear, echo through the woods, and echo out to wherever her father's first wife is buried, and her voice will lie down on top of the woman like a soft, warm blanket and stay there until the snowmelt in Spring.

THE CALIFORNIA WATER WAR

While his brother Felix is taking one last look across the valley to make sure no one is near, Guillermo lights the fuse and drops the stick of dynamite into the aqueduct.

"Let's go," Guillermo says, and he tries to hide his smile as Felix figures out what he's done.

When he does, Felix says, "Hey, it was my turn."

Felix is right of course, but what can he do? The fuse has been lit, and the stick has been dropped. Now they need to run like the white man who gave them the explosive said to, the man who had the idea that maybe little explosions could do as much as the big explosion the ranchers did last year. They're a good half-mile away out into the scrub when the thud comes echoing out to them, and they dive behind a bush just like the man told them to.

"You lit the last one."

And Felix got Delores. That's what Guillermo wants to say, but he just shrugs as best he can lying on his stomach. "Sorry. Next time."

They lie there, watching for fifteen minutes to make sure no one heard, and no one will come. The man said thirty minutes, but after fifteen, Guillermo starts to stand. Before he can get all the way up, Felix grabs his wrist and pulls him back to the dirt.

"Stay down." And Guillermo is going to thrash him, but he's pointing across the valley to a cowboy trotting toward where the explosion was. The cowboy is scanning the desert looking for people. The cowboy has a rifle.

"Is he alone?"

But Felix doesn't answer.

The cowboy walks to the spot where they dropped the stick and stares at it. After a minute, his head snaps up as though he heard something. He raises his rifle and shoots into the scrub, but it's nowhere near Guillermo and his brother.

They stare at him silently until he turns his back to them. "Delores is pregnant," Felix says.

Guillermo almost says, "Do you think it's yours?" Then he almost says, "Well, then she's a whore." Then his rage vibrates through his brain until it knocks his ideas loose, and all he can do is stare at the sandy dirt in front of his face and breathe. When he comes back to himself, he says, "When are you going to get married?"

"Tuesday. You'll be the best man." This is a big brother's order, not a question.

Guillermo lets the rage come and go again. He thinks about standing up and walking toward the cowboy. He will walk within rifle range and stand until he's shot down. He thinks about offering his death up for his brother so no one will think to hunt for Felix. There is a chance now that the cowboy will form a posse, and they'll both be caught and killed, but not if Guillermo offers up his life right now.

He thinks about Felix's wedding on Tuesday. They would have to delay it for Guillermo's funeral, and when people make speeches at the wedding, they would be about Guillermo and his courage. Delores would think about him, and Felix would cry, and everyone would know that she should have chosen him over his coward brother.

Instead of standing, though, he gets up on his hands and knees, and he hears Felix start to follow him. He wonders how far they'll have to travel like this before they can finally stand and walk like men. It will be miles, he thinks. Many, many miles.

HALCYON SOLSTICE

T HE SKY is soft mist. She knows that the night's conversation back and forth between sea and sand will leave wavy lines by daylight, commensurate with the moon, leave strands of the dream stories spelled out by amber kelp, rough like the blanket fibers covering the sleeping clan. Morning will come soon.

She tests the weight of the stone with her wrist, walks from the whisper water to the bluffs, and slips her hand inside the cave of the cyan-crested shorebird, the horizontal tunnel in the cliff dug by the male bird through the night.

Inside she slips the stone of cogs, turns its wheel to the morning star, removes the old bones left by bandit birds, then squats and scoops wet sand, rubs it across her forehead and scrapes two more handfuls, capsizes her hands and lets the sand run through, to honor. To turn the emptiness of one story into a bowl of light.

Sleeve of sand bluff, tunnel of shelter, burrowed as a nest but changed now to this. Arm's length into the depth, the full reach as far as the body will allow. How she loves her family, her clan. Like the nest floating on the sea.

TANNERITE

At first, Manny thinks Arturo is going to land in a scrubby bush as he takes a couple of steps backward. Part of him wants Arturo to get all scratched up, but Arturo seems to have a preternatural sense of when to stop, and then he runs forward, kicking up the sandy dirt of the high desert before he jumps on top of the three foot high pipeline that takes all of the water from the Owens Valley to Los Angeles.

He has his shotgun with him today. Arturo always does when they go out to the desert, and he pulls a pipe out of his pocket.

"What's that?" Manny asks.

Arturo makes his voice effeminate. "'What's that?' It's tannerite."

"What?" Manny asks, and he folds his arms over his chest.

"You didn't think I could make something like this did you?"

Manny didn't. Arturo has talked about making a bomb as long as he's known him, way back in high school when Manny'd thought of him as a kind of god come down to earth. Back then, Arturo's crazy energy would work its way through Manny, and when they were together they became more than they ever could be apart. When they played football that year, everyone called them the two horsemen of the apocalypse. When they were in high school, Arturo would show him bomb-making videos on the Internet and say that they could build one if they wanted to.

Only, he never did, and Manny never wanted him to. As they got older, he decided that Arturo really didn't have the patience to construct one.

Today, Manny supposes he was wrong about that.

"What are you going to do with that?"

"We're finally going to take this valley back." He's walking up and down the pipeline, stomping on it with his military surplus boots.

"I don't know what that means, Arturo."

"Everyone," he stops walking and points a finger at Manny, "everyone bitches about the water. No one ever does anything. When did everyone get to be such fucking cowards?"

Arturo places his homemade bomb on the metal of the pipeline.

"Tannerite's not like dynamite. We're not going to crater this, but water's going to come out of the hole, and it's going to flow into the valley where it's supposed to."

"You have to be kidding me." Something in Arturo's voice makes Manny take a couple of steps back until he steps into a bush.

Arturo sweeps his shotgun across the desert. "Everyone is going to know about this, and they're all going to know that I did it. When the valley fills up with water, and we have a lake again, you're going to tell them about what I did." Arturo gets a faraway look. "Maybe have someone write a song or something."

"Why don't you tell them yourself?" Manny asks, but he's taken a few more steps back. He can see what's going to happen, knows that Arturo is going to put the barrel of his shotgun against the tannerite bomb even before Arturo does it.

He doesn't bother trying to stop Arturo from pulling the trigger. He never could stop him from doing anything. The only thing he can do is help or get out of his way, and so he runs backward in big bouncing steps, watching his friend in the last reels of this moment.

DISHEVELED

"It looks like a bomb went off," Kate says when she first sees the damage.

The maps and atlases are among the bottom strata, along with the other books that were on the lowest shelves in each room. They will be the last to be picked up, having been covered by all of the volumes that tumbled from the shelves above. Everything is dusted with a white-gray powder of debris from the cracked ceilings and window casings.

"Like powdered sugar on a Bundt cake," Kate says. "The windows held. Unlike a lot of places. That's one thing to be grateful for."

"Epicenter was in Sylmar," Kevin says, entering with a tray of four lidded coffees in paper cups. He nods to Kate to grab one. "6.5 magnitude."

"You're a life saver. Thanks, Kev." She wriggles a cup from the holder, then squints as she sips, surveying the room. "We're going to need more than this."

"I should have brought beer," Kevin says dryly.

"After five. For sure."

"More like after ten. Maybe eleven."

Stella sighs. "We just don't have the budget for this. With all of the cuts, we're to the bone just keeping the doors open, even with our reduced hours." She sets her coffee down on the circulation desk. "No one planned for this."

"How can anyone plan for this?" Kate says.

Kevin's blue eyes sparkle, holding back a laugh. "How can anyone not?" She frowns at him, not getting it. "Well, it's not like this is the first earthquake to shake L.A."

Stella looks to Kevin flatly, too heavy in the heart to consider the humor. "I'll have to appeal for emergency funding."

"I thought you said there isn't any," Kate says.

"There isn't."

By eight that evening, based on the progress made by that day's regular staff, Stella has calculated the hours it will take to re-shelf the 400,000 volumes. She types the numbers in a memo flagged "URGENT" and uses the small white-out brush to cover "man hours" before retyping "hours of labor" in the thicker, softer island of white. She leans in and blows on it to clear away some pebbly specks from the place of repair, then thinks of how that gesture is a microcosm for the enormous task that remains in every room of the building she sits in. She sobs into her hands. Long and hard. Every time she thinks she's finished, she starts in again. She can't stop.

The next morning she is there first, and greets Kate and Kevin as they enter by extending a tray of coffees. "My turn."

"Thanks, Stell." Kevin hold out a large pink box of donuts. "Breakfast of Champions."

"Make me young," Kate says. "Make me young..."

Stella rubs her eye with her knuckle then looks around the main room, which has been cleared of the top layer of dust and debris for the most part, but almost all of the books are still on the floor.

"So, I wrote a memo to Alberta late last night. Called her on the phone, too."

Kate raises her eyebrows. Kevin can see that Stella doesn't want to tell them the rest.

"And?" Kate asks, finally.

"I called for volunteers from the community to come help us."

"No," Kate says. She looks to Kevin, widening her eyes.

"Stella Bella, there's a reason we have signs everywhere telling people to put their books on the carts and not to re-shelve them. They're worse than drunk monkeys on chandeliers tossing shit everywhere. It'll be a mess."

"It is a mess," she replies softly, not taking her gaze away from the long piles of books running like mountain ranges between the tall shelves. "We have no choice."

But later that morning, that same room is filled with bustling humanity, people stooping and wiping and calling off numbers from the spines as they hand the books to others who are meticulously sliding them back into order on the shelves. When Peter arrives, without Ramon, Kevin hands him a brush and dustpan before he can even wash up in the restroom. "Morning, Peter. Get a bed last night?"

Peter nods.

"I heard the Mission ceiling collapsed. Terrible. Glad to see you're okay." He shakes his head, looking up at the library ceiling. "Gonna be a lot of people out on the streets tonight."

Peter is flooded by an enormous sadness when he sees all of the books fallen and open. Something about it reminds him of things he saw in 'Nam, and something is reminiscent of the bodies he's seen out on the streets. He's deeply moved, too, by the sight of all of the people who have come to help, to pick up what has fallen, to make things better. Despite the debris, the rooms are crowded and bustling. All of the morning regulars are here, but Peter also notices some faces he's seen elsewhere. Business owners and shop workers. He recognizes several police officers, but in street clothes, and laughing. There is a large group of women with baby strollers. Dozens of high school girls in uniform, older well-dressed ladies with silver-blue hair, nuns in full garb, kids in wheelchairs, long-haired musicians, tattooed gang members, men in suits, construction workers, housewives, homeless. People from every nation on earth, Peter thinks. He then notices several different languages being spoken, and that makes him think of how these people are similar to the books themselves, how they all traveled here individually, and how the authors, too, came to assemble here through the years, one by one, how their stories are continuously being taken in, one book at a time, one line at a time, becoming part of someone else then, how they are lifted up into the light. Peter imagines all of the fingerprints placed along the spines through the years, including today, and all of the stories here, and for the first time in years, Peter is flooded with both hope and happiness.

That evening, Stella has similar thoughts as she sits at her desk and types another memo, this one reporting back on the remarkable progress made. All of the dust and debris has been cleaned in record time, she types, well ahead of the previous estimate, and the books, somehow, have been re-shelved. The maps and atlases and all other volumes from the lower shelves had kept their order for the most part, Stella explains, and by they time the volunteers got to those last ones, the last of the re-shelving was far easier and faster, but how at first it was slow going as those on top of the piles were terribly mixed up, having tumbled from shelving on both sides of the aisle and into central heaps of absolute chaos. Stella types that she is a bit ashamed how she had previously underestimated people's abilities and generosity, how the volunteers had proved beyond capable, how they streamed in all day, especially at lunch hour, workers skipping their meals to help however they could. She proposes that the Public Libraries create a proclamation or plaque commemorating the library patrons for their work in this time of crisis, noting how they were both efficient and accurate in the placing of the books in proper sequence and restoring the library back to working order. She wishes to add that the spirit of the volunteers was just as important in the restoration of the library, and that the mood remained positive, and that the people were actually singing by day's end, and Stella then related an anecdote of how the Gay Men's Chorus of Los Angeles and the First Baptist church choir at one point traded show tunes and gospel songs. Stella explains that at first volunteers headed toward their favorite genre, but that eventually people migrated across the library so that all day new friends were being made in every section. She stops to wipe her cheeks. Stella then ends the memo by noting how the volunteers continued to stream in all day, that once everything was put back, how she delegated volunteers to check that all had been placed in the proper Dewey Decimal order, how the volunteers then went book by book, row by row, and reported back that they had been correctly filed 99% of the time, and that those that hadn't were easily moved to the proper place. Stella writes that the order was then triple-checked by volunteers who came even later to help, and that there was no doubt in her mind that the holdings of the Los Angeles Public Library have never been in such perfect order thanks to her patrons. Stella ends the memo by noting that the volunteers continued to arrive well into the evening, just as eager to contribute as the first arrivals, and that they were told there was nothing for them to do other than to enjoy their library—their own public library.

SMELLING MARCH

These days when the cyan bird returns are the days the seas are calm. The full cycle of the moon is the reason she walks. The warm evening's shoreline solace. She thinks of the stone's quarter click in the cliff above her, the familiar bank of bluff mirroring the curve of shore. Here the warning sounds of strangers come easily on the wind. Inland march of clouds each morning clearing all, smelling of salt, carrying the promise of more. Walked banks. Return of green. Calmer nights. Solace sounds curve more moon.

THE SAN FRANCISCO EARTHQUAKE, 1906

When Mario sees the thousand smoke plumes rising he thinks of Teresa, who works for a fishmonger in a building overlooking the bay, and he is filled with the sudden understanding that in this entire world, she is the only thing that matters to him.

Out here, on the ocean, even all these miles out, the city looks ransacked, destroyed by Huns or Mongols. His brother Anthony crosses himself and says, "God has fulfilled the gift prophesied in *Revelation*." Anthony has spent a lot of his time lately looking around for signs of the end. He sees them in the waves and in the way birds flock. He points them out to Mario in the newspaper whenever they are ashore. Mario has kept Teresa the secret of his heart because he knows that his brother will talk about the sin. He will speak of lust, so Mario will not tell anyone about her until he asks for her hand.

When Anthony starts to pray the rosary, Mario wonders if he is sorry that he missed his apocalypse. His first mate is lost, he knows, at least for fifteen minutes, but then Anthony apparently decides he is going to do all fifteen decades of the rosary. When he starts into the sixth decade, Mario says, "Shut up with that for now."

Anthony turns to him. "What did you say?"

"On this boat, I am your God. Do your job." There is only so much wind, but today, Mario will use it as he never has before.

Anthony smirks at Mario as if he knows something. Anthony always smirks like that, but today Mario has to look away. "If God has lain waste to San Francisco for its sins, maybe it is better that we find a different port."

"If God were going to destroy the world, he wouldn't forget the fishermen." He wants to gut Anthony with his knife. He wants to throw him over the side of the boat and watch him freeze to death.

"You see with your own eyes the new Sodom destroyed by God's wrath, and still you disbelieve."

Anthony is the little brother, but Mario has not stood up to him since they have become adults. Everyone knows that Anthony's religion makes him the better brother, the wiser brother, but when he thinks of Teresa, he says, "What I see is that the city has been burned down, and I think that we might be able to help some people."

He turns to Anthony who opens his mouth to speak but cannot seem to find any words to fit the moment.

"I am still the captain," Mario says.

Closer to the city, they can see that the people have not been turned to salt. They are walking along the shore, busy in their own lives. The people, many of them at least, have survived, but so many of the buildings that lie in the city are cracked apart or are simply gone like the teeth of an old drunk. It is not until they are in the bay that they smell the world burned now down to its studs. Mario steers his little boat into the bay and around the other side, and as they come around past Alcatraz Island, he hears his brother sigh.

"What's wrong?"

"It takes so long to be called back to his kingdom."

"I can shorten the trip for you."

"You're the captain of your little skiff, Primo, but that doesn't mean that you can talk to me any way that you want to."

Mario points to the city. "You see that, and you still feel sorry for yourself."

Anthony smiles. "I'm thinking with my soul. You're thinking

with that." He nods at Mario's crotch, and there is nothing for Mario to say. Somehow, Anthony knows about his secret. Somehow, his little brother has looked into his heart. "Do you really think your little prostitute has been thinking about you through all of this?"

"I wouldn't talk about Teresa if I were you."

"I wouldn't think about her if I were you. God hates the sin of entertaining lustful thoughts, and I do too."

Mario leaves the wheel, grabs his little brother with one hand under his armpit, and throws him into the cold bay. He does it without thinking, but it brings him joy when it's done. Anthony splashes and curses at him, and Mario thinks he will probably live. The water is cold, but they are only a hundred yards from shore. If he dies, that would be fine too.

As he comes around to his dock, he thinks about Teresa and his brother's ridiculous idea of the apocalypse, both of those things at the same time, and it makes him want to laugh at his brother. Except that from here, Mario can see the burned-out building where Teresa used to sell her fish. God in his wisdom has chosen to blot it out. Where it once stood, now there is a moment of black soot, and she is either dead or wandering the city, another Teresa splashing around in an ocean of Teresas.

Mario stares at the apocalypse of the fish store, and he wonders about Anthony's dream of Revelation. May it come soon. May it be hard. May it burn out the memory of what was here yesterday and what has become of today.

EUREKA

When we fall fast, it is easier for not having to face a long goodbye, she thinks.

But harder for not being able to say goodbye. "Which is why we need to make things clear now," she says. "Yes. That's what we need to do." She wipes her cheek with her knuckle and nods, as if assuring herself.

"What?"

"We need to make things clear now."

He looks down to his lap, his peripheral vision catching her shape behind him on the bed. That was as far as he could look.

"Okay?"

He softens. "Okay."

Earlier, long before he had known she was watching him, he sat on the edge of the bed and stared out the window to watch the sunrise. She watched him watching the sky lighten, his face lightening with it in the dark room. She imagined what he was seeing. That familiar tree line. The colorful sky he would soon be traveling through. After all, she knew she would be staring at that scene later, once he left. And in the slow days after. The next day. She would be able to look at that view from the bedroom whenever she wanted. But he —

"When my dog was dying..."

She blinks him back into focus. "What, hon?"

"I laid with him all night."

His voice is a faint cloud, like the ones he had pointed out earlier in the day. Barely there and so far up.

"I'm sorry, hon. What about the night?"

"I couldn't sleep, so..."

"Me neither."

"So..." He thinks of stroking that fine silver hair on his dog's neck, his other arm tucked under him like a pillow, his dog nuzzling his nose deep into his curled hand and breathing heavily. His flick-paw dreams, that might have awakened him had he not already been awake all night as he tried to take it all in. It was—what? Devastatingly sad, yes, but reassuring. There had to be a word for that emotion. Like those clouds so high up. Pale white. Surrounded by blue, with blue showing through, but holding on to their color as they thin. Knowing his dog could sleep at last cleared the way for him to sleep a bit, too. But he stayed awake, not wanting to miss anything, now that their time was so short. Saying to himself: remember this moment, right now. Trying to notice the details he often overlooked. Trying to make it stick. As close to stopping time as he could get. This. Which was something like forever, he supposed. Those moments when time slipped the tracks and left things suspended and all at once.

"So..." she whispers back.

INTERNAL INJURIES

THE POLICE scanner has been broadcasting only static for several minutes now, but the last word was that the fire was still on the other side of the ridge, though the winds were picking up again. Early that morning, the firefighter from Laguna Beach Fire Station Number 2 who came to the door said that the wind had died down through the night, so now they were at 50% containment, but that it was still recommended they leave if they had another place to go to until tomorrow. Evacuation was not yet mandatory, but would be if the fire got much closer.

Six hours later the air is thick, the late afternoon light orangeish and diffused, lacking shadows. Whispers of static from the radio alternate from loud to soft, loud to soft, in slow pulsing cycles, like the surf.

The woman looks at the man sitting in the chair a few feet to her left, then looks down. *Oh—* She begins to smooth the white napkin spread on her lap, her open palms pressing wrinkles down as if ironing the boy's shirt. *He'll need this for school in the morning.* She hums softly. She smells— *What is that? Burning newspapers?*

Then a crash and the window in the next room shatters.

Oh! A shush of glass as it scatters across the tile floor. *Has the child run into the slider? Oh dear!* Her heartbeat is suddenly shooshing in her ears and her face grows hot.

And with that, a full-grown deer bolts into the room.

Her hands clutch fistfuls of napkin and cotton dress, and the man's fingers dig into the leather arms of the recliner as he presses himself back with straightened arms. The buck, likewise, stiffens its legs, cloven hooves skidding on the hardwood. Wild crescents of white fear flash around brown irises. The buck scrambles to maintain his balance, then in an instant stands rigid, frozen but for his heavy panting, his sides flexing in out, in out. The man's eyes are drawn to the crimson gash that glistens diagonally across the muscular neck. Then he scans the beast from the large antlers down to the liquid eye, the flaring nostril, then follows the gash to the line of blood streaming down the front leg. The buck snorts loudly, then lets out a quick raspy cough as he swings his head high.

"Jesus!" the man cries. The buck's ears twitch and rotate to the sound at once, and he swings his head now to lock eyes with the man. The two hold stares for a few shortened breaths, time slowing for both of them, as if they are in some other realm together, bonded. When the woman starts tapping her feet, both the man and the deer look over to her shoes, but the man looks back to the gash that flickers light now. The edges reveal the thickness of skin and puffy fat beneath, sliced clean and straight as if guided by the hand of some skilled surgeon. *Well there it is,* the man thinks. *He's going to die.* He inhales and holds his breath for a beat. *Put him out of his misery.*

And with that the deer shakes his head, spraying blood. The woman flinches. *Oh!—* The deer swings his head toward her. The man looks over to see his wife returning the deer's gaze with moist eyes. Her is face calm. They seem bonded. She looks to him as if she might be lucid for a moment, appears almost holy sitting there.

"Ma?"

And with that the buck bolts, or tries to, his hooves bunching the island of rug by the armoire. He scrambles through the entryway and the man thinks he is going to run down the hall into their bedroom, but instead the buck, having gained firmer footing on the carpet now, in one motion spins, crouches, and bounds through the picture window, shattering it in a cloud of glass slivers, the curtain left trailing through the splintered hole to the outside world.

"Jesus H!" the man blurts, springing to his feet. He runs to the front window just in time to see the tan hind with white tail disappear over the hedges. It is heading downhill, through the diffused light toward the ocean. The man hurries back across the room, passes in front of his wife without looking at her. In the kitchen he kicks a few small squares of green-tinted glass, their kitchen window now relocated across the floor in thick cube-like chunks like a shattered windshield. The man follows drops of blood back to the thick, dark puddle where the buck had stood in front of their chairs. His wife sits, head down, smoothing the napkin on her lap and humming to herself.

"Come on, Ma. Get up."

He always calls her Ma, though they never had children. The first time was on their wedding day, right after the priest had said, "I now pronounce you..." He had kissed her, jerked his head toward the aisle and said it for the first time: "Let's go, Ma."

And she had blushed and slapped his chest, afraid someone might misinterpret the "Ma" and think perhaps... But she wasn't. Not yet. And so he had continued to call her that, even though.... How often he thought in these past several months how peculiar life is, how a simple phrase said off the cuff can have hidden in it the full arc of a lifetime to come, how an innocent gesture made without thinking can be a seed that alters all that comes after, growing in importance until it possesses enough weight to carve a new shape in the sky, how it seems sometimes that our words really do create our world, and how other times when the plan doesn't hold, those same words embed themselves deep within and act instead like a ballast to slow what once flowed so freely. She was "Ma" to him from that day forward, yes, in sickness and in health, and it was true that she quickly grew to love that term of endearment. "Okay, Pa," she began to say back to him, and they would grin and link arms, lean into each other then step out together, wherever it was they were headed.

"Come on, Ma! Get up. We gotta find him. Help him if we can.

He's hurt."

The boy! she thinks.

He thinks he sees something awakening now, and he reaches out his hand to her. But she ignores it, instead looking past him at the curtain pouring out like a stream of water through the jagged glass opening. She frowns. Nothing is making sense. She is frightened.

The man walks quickly to closet, grabs each of their coats, thinking to himself all the while how afraid he has become lately the more silent she's become. She's already left on a trip ahead of him, he sometimes thinks, but he doesn't want to lose her in the flesh too, doesn't want to be left to live alone, awaken one morning to find an empty shell in the sheets beside him, her beautiful pale blue eyes softened to dullness. No, he doesn't want to follow her down that road too, the both of them sinking into dusk, helpless. Staccato honks of a car alarm in the distance wipes the thought, and he quickly shrugs his coat on and walks back to his wife.

He helps her to her feet, holds her coat open, and she slides into it in one motion, like she's making a dance move. He thinks he sees her grin slightly, too. He's grateful for those small things she still can do without much prompting, and he half-brushes, half-pats a grey hair away from her collar and kisses the shoulder of her coat from behind. Then he hooks her arm and leads her outside, down their walkway and through the trellis archway.

The street runs downhill all the way to PCH, the beach on the other side, several hundred steps away. No sign of trouble, but a squeal of tires tells him the deer is probably crossing the highway, and he hunches his shoulders and waits for the sound of an impact, but none comes. He exhales loudly, then turns the other way and looks uphill. No flames yet. Perhaps everything is going to be okay after all.

They are both out of breath when they get to the foot of the hill. The man pats his wife's forearm and nods. Her cheekbones are flushed pink, the thin white skin at her temples pulsing. She is looking at the back of her hands now, confused.

"I'm sorry we went so fast, Ma. We'll slow down from here. You okay?"

The woman looks up at the man and he is looking intensely at her, from one eye to the other. Is she in trouble now? He leans back and smiles and she raises her brows. He slowly lifts her hand by her fingers and she feels her face grow hot as he kisses the back of her knuckles. *How bold!* But he hooks her arm now in his with such confidence it all seems familiar, reassuring, and she follows his lead as he steps forward and they cross the street to the parking lot.

Just then, a young couple, hand in hand, trot playfully past them, heading toward the ocean. A Mercedes squeals into the parking lot and screeches to a halt, and a man in a business suit hops out and begins running in the same direction.

"Here, let's take off your shoes, Ma."

She blushes as the bold man kneels before her and carefully slips each shoe off. As he begins to unlaced his own, she looks around, embarrassed that anyone might think he was crazy kneeling there like that. She wants laugh, but also wants to cry.

The man stands back up with a groan and helps his wife step over the curbing and into the sand, and he loops her arm again and walks her slowly toward the surf, both pairs of shoes swinging by their laces from his left wrist. It's been years since they walked in the sand. He can't even remember.

By the time they get to the water they are both breathing hard, the crisp salt air stinging their nostrils. The young couple stands on tip-toes, their slender hands held flat to shield their eyes as they stare out at the water, the girl bouncing slightly every few moments. The businessman stands behind the girl, eyeing her slim waist and the bones of her back. Fifty yards farther down the shore two young boys laugh and shout words that become jibberish by the time the wind tumbles them down the beach to where the crowd now stands, focused on the water.

"I don't see it!" the girl whines. "Where?" She hops up and down.

"There!" the young man shouts, and thrusts his hand out, pointing. "Beyond the waves. See his antlers? Oh my god! Oh my god, he's swimming out to sea!"

A yellow jeep roars up, its thick tires spraying the wet sand along the water's edge. It skids to a stop in front of the crowd. A muscular man in red trunks leaps onto the sand just before the jeep stops, and he scrambles to the back and begins digging for something. The driver, also in red trunks, thinner and much older, slithers up to stand on his seat, brings a large pair of binoculars to his eyes. He scans the water beyond the breakers, all business.

"He's right there!" the young man shouts from behind. Without turning or lowering the binoculars, the man in the jeep calmly replies, "I see him." All eyes follow the direction his goggles seem to point, straining to find the injured deer in the waves.

Without moving his locked gaze, the lifeguard drops his binoculars onto the seat, leaps off the truck and sprints into the surf. His younger partner lifts two paddle boards and a thick loop of rope out of the back of the jeep and follows, knees lifting high as he splashes through the foam.

"They're going after it! They're going to try to save him!" the young girl screams, raising her hands to the sky.

And with that the old man, whose eyes were lost along the line of the horizon, hears his own thin voice at fourteen years, crying out, "Let me go! I gotta save him!"

PRAISING STRANGE GODS

THE CHURCH father tells them that they need to remove the blanket of new earth brought by the floods, that it will expose the ancestors who now sleep in the quite place, so they will all need to travel to a new home. He explains how they must be the ones to dig, to accompany them on their journey, but that he will offer prayers and blessings so that their travels will be safe and that the new resting place of their ancestors will be watched over by God. She wonders which god, and how he could know such a thing. She thinks of the future without the ancestors here, how this place will look. How they too may soon be forced to move away. How strange it would be to sleep forever in a different place than this, their home. She thinks of what this place might turn into. How people will forget their lives, forget their stories, forget what is sacred. She thinks about how strange new things will flood this place. Strange new people praising strange gods.

PART SIX
DRIVING WEDGES

"We can't let people drive wedges between us… because there's only one human race."

— Dolores Huerta

HOWARD'S MAGIC

When Howard comes home in the evening, he tells everyone that there's a television show on tonight that he wants them all to watch. "It'll explain what I'm doing all day long at work." He takes a shuddering breath. "It'll explain why I'm doing it, too."

"Joe's taking me out tonight," Beverly says in a whine.

June is willing to watch it with him, even excited in her way, but she understands why her daughter doesn't want to.

Howard clears his throat and extends the moment by taking a sip of his coffee. "Joe can take you out any night."

June rubs her husband's leg. "Howard, it's her first date. Let her go."

Something about this program is important to him. Something beyond what he's told them, and she can feel the anger starting to heat up inside of him.

"It's important," he says.

"I thought we could have a private conversation after the show." It's their code for having sex, and although June's not in the mood, she's less in the mood for a fight, especially about something like a first date.

So Howard sits a little straighter and says, "Your first date, huh?"

"Yeah. Joe chose me," Beverly says and goes into a long nattering conversation about Joe who is a hero of her high school apparently and a couple years older than her daughter, and June thinks that she should probably be concerned, but she isn't. She tunes out what her daughter is telling her husband and thinks about her own first date, which was with Howard in 1945 and led in very short order to Beverly. She thinks about how nice that night was, and though Beverly meant the end of college and everything she had hoped for, how none of that matters now.

After dinner and after Joe picks up Beverly, and June assures Howard that he looks like such a nice boy, he sits her down, makes sure she's paying attention and turns on a news program that they never watch, and she realizes immediately why he's so excited about it. The television crew has traveled out to the New Mexico base that Howard visits every month or so. Most of the time, he's here in California in front of a drafting desk, but on the program they're in front of the desert scenery he's always describing. He talks about how empty it is, and how it seems clean after the blasts.

"It's like after Noah's flood, only better."

The news crew goes through the base interviewing the people the government has given them permission to interview, filming scientists who tell them how safe the bombs are for Americans and filming politicians who tell them how dangerous they are for the Soviets. At one point, they go into a laboratory.

"This is it," Howard says, and he catches his breath a little. "Right here."

He crouch-walks off the couch and up to the television set. When the scene switches to a group of important looking engineers in masks and white hooded suits, he points to the third one on the left. "That's me," he says, tapping the glass.

"That's your God-damn husband."

It's the first time he's sworn in the sixteen years she's known him, and he beams at her, clearly unaware that he's done it. When he sits back down, the scene changes again to a countdown and then a bomb going off in the distance and then a slow-motion view of what it's like in the middle of a nuclear explosion, and Howard is saying, "I did that. I did that." June pushes out a smile as hard as she can like she's working a splinter out of the palm of her hand. Afterward, he does his business with her triumphantly and doesn't seem to notice that she's quiet.

Not that she wants him to notice.

She stays in bed when he goes out to the living room to wait up for Beverly, and she weeps to herself silently. She wants to fall asleep, but she lies there with her eyes staring up at the ceiling and thinking about that house in Howard's program, the one that sways back and forth in the nuclear breeze a couple of times before it is torn off its foundation. Howard did that. That was his magic.

She's still awake when Beverly comes home, and she hears Howard say, "You should've been here. You should have seen it."

She can't hear Beverly's thin words though all that drywall, but she hears the joy in her voice. She hears the hope. That hope makes her get out of bed and put on her robe. She comes downstairs to see Beverly on the couch and Howard standing in front of her, talking with his arms.

"You don't get it. Your old man was on television. They showed what I do every day. They talked about me like I'm a hero."

June rubs his shoulder. "You are a hero, Darling."

Howard beams at the praise and kisses her. She thinks about that first date and what they did tonight, and how it was all fine, but none of it really matters.

"How was your night, Bev?" she asks.

"It was swell." Howard might not notice. How could he on a night like tonight, when the famous news reporter, John Cameron Swayze, praised him specifically? But June can see the electricity running through her daughter. She wonders what happened and how far Beverly went with this boy.

"Swell?" Howard asks. He pets his daughter's hair. "That boy doesn't know how lucky he is."

Later, June comes into Beverly's bathroom as she's washing her face. "I want to hear about the date. All of it."

Beverly cocks her head. "He shook my hand at the end of the night," she says.

"You sound disappointed."

"I wanted him to kiss me. I wanted him to hold me." She sounds to June like she's straight out of one of those terrible teen movies that she's always going to with Beverly. "Is that wrong of me?"

"No, not at all."

"How do I get him to do it?"

She wants to tell her daughter, not to move so slowly. She wants to tell her that if she takes her man in her mouth, it will drive him mad, and that he will love her and take her, and she'll feel that someone in this world is overwhelmed by an unspeakable need for her. She wants to tell her not to wait because her father is a magician, and they have maybe one or two good years before his sorcery wipes the entire world smooth, but she doesn't have the words for any of that.

"Lean in close to him," she says instead. "Then he'll have to hold you."

This is good enough, she supposes, and maybe it will lead to the other. The holding is the best part anyway, that feeling that she is safe and loved and always will be.

THE BEAUTY OF A BETTIE PAGE HAIRCUT

Most of the kids at Artie's high school are scared by the film Mr. Meyers plays in class, the one where the atom bomb goes off and blasts the fake town the government built in the middle of the California or Nevada desert. One girl even cries. Artie can see its beauty. This is going to save the world from itself, and two minutes after Meyers turns off the projector, Artie knows what he's going to do with the rest of his life.

On Saturday, he takes his bike downtown to the recruiter's office. He walks in smoking a cigarette and wearing sunglasses, but the old guy behind the desk isn't fooled and tells him to come back when he's old enough to grow a mustache.

Outside the office, he decides it's a good thing. If he really wants to work on the nukes, he needs to go out west, so he waits until his dad is down at the movie theater, and he goes to the highway and sticks out his thumb. A week later, he's trudging through the Oregon fog when he sees the sign that tells him he's finally crossed over into California.

There on the side of the road he starts singing, "California Here I Come," and doing a little dance, laughing until he hears an engine coming. When he does, he sits down on the side of the road and hangs his head like he's nearly dead. His week's worth of experience has taught him how to make sure anyone will stop for him.

It's a woman who stops, a girl really, by herself in a pickup truck, the first time that's happened. She says hello, and he says he's going south as far as she'll take him. She says that's all right, but she's going to need money for gas or they're not going far. She looks a little bit like Bettie Page, which gets him thinking or rather, not thinking, and he asks her name, and she says,

"Candace."

"Not Candy?"

She turns in her seat and stares at him, not answering for a moment. "Does your mother know you're out here?" It's a funny kind of thing to say because she might be older than he is but not by much.

"I doubt it," and he does. Artie is the only person he knows whose mother died in the war in Europe. When the recruiters told his father that his asthma meant that he couldn't sign up, his mother went to be a nurse. He remembers when they got the letter. She had been in Ardennes. He takes out a cigarette and lights it up. Everyone always looks older smoking. "Where are you going?" he asks.

"Tonight, probably Eureka. Tomorrow, San Francisco, I hope. If I can make it. You going that far?"

He snorts a laugh. "San Francisco? No." He's heard the stories about what kind of people they have down there and what kinds of things they do. "I'm going to Sacramento, I think."

"What's there?"

He takes a long drag on his cigarette and exhales, lets the smoke cloud around his head. "I'm going to sign up."

"What, for the army?"

"Sure," he says, "do my bit." No one says that anymore, he knows, but he likes the sound of it.

"You have to be kidding me. How old are you?"

"How old do you think I am?"

"Fifteen going on twelve."

He's spent the last week letting his facial hair grow out, but it's come in two clumps. Maybe it'd be better to shave it off. "Nah," he says. "I just turned eighteen."

"Yeah right. You're not ready for the army yet."

"I had an uncle who signed up to go to Germany when he was sixteen."

"So that's your real age then, sixteen?"

"Seventeen," he says, "and a half." He takes another puff and contemplates the foggy world outside. "You don't think they're going to let me in? I mean, if I found the right recruiter, don't you think they'd take me?"

She considers it a little, stares out at the trees that are passing. "Actually, I bet there's someone who'd take you, especially now, but you don't want to join up. Truman's going to get us into Korea."

"You mean like a war?"

She stares at him blankly for a moment. "Yeah, like a war."

This makes him laugh again. "We're not going to fight anyone."

"What makes you think that?"

"We got the nukes. We're never going to have another war ever again. I mean, who's going to fight us when we've got bombs like that." She's like everyone else in this world, scared about all the wrong things. "I'm going to sign up, and they're going to put me to work on them."

"On the nukes?"

Instead of answering, he takes a drag and smiles. He lets the smoke out slowly, trying to make a mushroom cloud but failing. It's all right. He's going to learn how. Maybe get a tattoo of one too.

"Listen, why don't you just come with me to San Francisco for a couple of weeks and think about it? I'm going to dorm there. You can stay with me for free. I bet I can sneak you in at night. I'll introduce you to some kids our age." She rubs the corner of her eye, and he thinks maybe it's a tear, but that doesn't make sense.

"Nah, thank you." Her face tells him she's serious. It's kind of great, actually, having this Bettie Page looking girl all concerned about him. He wonders how much of her body looks like Bettie's.

He wonders what her skin feels like, if she's turned on by a uniform. "There'd have to be a good reason for me to ever go to San Francisco." He puts emphasis on the word, "good."

"Good reason? Free rent." She takes a deep breath, and lets it out all uneven. "I've known kids like you who signed up."

"Yeah? Like who?"

"Like my brother and his friend. It's almost ten years later, and my brother still hasn't gotten out of his hospital bed and his friend's dead. My father died too, and my mother..." She doesn't finish the sentence. Instead, she starts crying for real not like she's sad but gone all hysterical with fear for him. She takes out a hanky and dabs at her face.

"Don't cry. That's not such a bad way to go out. It's the way I want to die. Besides, like I said, it's a different world now. No more war."

That makes her choke on a sob, and Artie reaches out to comfort her, touches her shoulder. When she gets control over herself a little, she says, "Please, just come to San Francisco with me, just for a couple of weeks and think about it."

He doesn't want to hurt her, but he was serious. "I don't think so. I'd really have to have a good reason to go there."

She turns and stares at him, her face twisted up. A logging truck comes out of the fog in the oncoming lane and passes them, but she doesn't even seem to notice. "Fine," she says.

"Fine what?"

"Come with me to San Francisco. You can do anything you want to me. I'll be with you. I'll give you whatever you want."

"Really?"

"Really, really."

He wonders how much she actually believes what she's saying, but he can see that she's trying to keep from weeping again. He wonders if he could actually talk her into making love to him.

He thinks about the nukes and how if they'd had them his mother would be alive today. He thinks about Bettie Page and the hours he's spent dreaming about her, but he knows that not even Candace can keep him from this path.

"Look, you don't even have to decide yet," she says. "Stay with me tonight in Eureka, and then choose tomorrow. I'll even drive you to Sacramento if you want me to."

"All right," he says, and he knows that this is a great new world.

Everything is spread out in front of him, and all he has to do is reach out his hand. The world's been made whole by these genius scientists in California, and he's going to join them. He's going to save this precious world, make it right for the mothers, the brothers, the fathers, their sons.

THE SNAKE

Lynda and Tom wait in their car in the hundred degree heat until the postman stuffs the mailbox with envelopes and drives around the corner. Lynda watches silently as Tom lights a cigarette and takes the cardboard box in the backseat across the street. He doesn't look out for anyone, but that's her job, and no one seems to be around. So she lets him open the mailbox and slide the rattlesnake into it. When it's well in, he slams the door and knocks on the metal a few times, the banging echoing up and down the street.

Back in the car, he takes a drag, licks his teeth, and asks, "So you wanna see a movie?"

Lynda shrugs. "Sure." She says this like it's nothing, like she doesn't want to puke from fear and guilt. He fires up the car and wheels around the corner. "There's a new one with Marilyn." When he scowls, she says, "There's a John Wayne film, too."

"Either way," he says. "I don't care."

They drive silently for a time until at a stop sign, she says, "What if they send the little boy out to get the mail?"

"Well, then he'll get bit."

She can feel the tears coming even though she knows how much he hates them. She can stop them mostly unless they come in a big rush.

He sighs. "Most people don't die from a rattler bite. If the kid gets bit, they'll go to the hospital and get him fixed up." He takes another drag of the cigarette. "And I promise you if that happens, they'll move out of here fast."

He looks left and right, always the careful driver.

"But what if he dies."

"He's not going to die. I promise."

"But what if he does?"

Tom sucks the last of his cigarette and flicks it out the window. "If he dies, then maybe that's for the best." He pulls another cigarette from the pack and lights it with his left hand.

"You don't mean that."

Tom gets that serious and thoughtful face. "It's hard, I know. But I'd rather one of their kids die than one of ours. They should have moved down to Pomona. You know that."

"But he could die."

"If one of them moves in, then the rest follow, and soon the town will be full of drugs and knives and you know that our kids are going to be the ones who suffer. Anyway, they're happier this way among their own kind."

That's when the tears come, and Lynda finds herself crying into her hands. She can't help it, can't stop, but he doesn't yell at her this time. He pulls over to the side of the road and takes her into his arms and just lets her cry it out.

When she slows down a little, she says, "But what if someone saw you. I can't watch you go to prison."

He squeezes her hard. "I hate this too, but it has to be done, and no one but me is going to do it. I didn't fight a war to come home and see my town run down."

She pulls back a little just to look at his face, which is at peace, which is calm. This man, she knows, would sacrifice anything for her and the kids. This man would walk through hell fire. This man is the very definition of love.

He takes a drag on his cigarette and licks his teeth.

MARATHON MAN

Gareth takes his wife to see *Marathon Man* and loves it except for the scene when Szell, the former Nazi, is seen by a survivor in New York, and she points at him and screams for help. It feels right that he's been found out, but he feels pity too and something else. It doesn't quite seem fair to him. That was the war and this is now.

He mentions that feeling to his wife, but she doesn't get him. She never has.

He thinks about his time during WWII as a guard in the internment camp when he watched all the Japanese. It was light duty compared to what some guys had, but he wonders now what would happen if he walked into the wrong part of San Francisco or Los Angeles. Would someone point at him and start to scream? He thinks about those years of blowing cold and the summer's unending heat. He thinks about the riot and firing his rifle. He thinks about the killed and the wounded. It's not the same as what happened in Germany, he knows. It's not even close. Still.

Gareth finds himself driving on the freeway on Saturday morning before anyone else is really awake in the city. At first, he's not sure where he's going, but slowly, it dawns on him that he's headed in the general direction of Chinatown. He gets out on Hill and College and walks the streets that are just beginning to fill with people.

He wonders if there are any Japanese mixed in with the Chinese. He wonders where they moved to when he was sent back home. He spends the morning wandering the street, making eye contact with people wondering if he'll remember faces from thirty years ago, wondering if they'll remember him.

When he comes home, his wife asks him where he's been all morning, and he tells her that she wouldn't understand. She wouldn't either. Neither would the Marathon Man or the people he guarded all those years ago. Maybe he thinks, Szell would understand him and what he's begun to feel this last week. Maybe there is a real life Szell out there to talk to, but he just doesn't know.

He thinks about pointing his rifle at those people. He thinks about the pressure against his shoulder each time he pulled the trigger. He thinks about late nights in the guard tower when he would get bored and aim his rifle at people's windows. He thinks about how he laughed. He thinks about the long daydreams of his youth.

THE VIEW FROM THE MONKEY BARS

When the nuclear air raid siren starts, Tanya can feel her breath stop, and she turns to Katie to see if she needs to start crying, but Katie's face is asking the same question. She and Katie and all of the other kids turn to Mrs. Hoover who is smiling and waving, letting everyone know that this is just the monthly test.

The boys on the field stop their games and start throwing their bodies into the air and onto the ground as though they're being blown up. Tanya keeps her eyes on Damien Carson who is dying painfully in front of Miss Hoover. He's melting slowly into the ground, begging her desperately to save him, but she only shakes her head. When he weeps to his teacher, she laughs so hard she has to cover her mouth. How can she not see how beautiful this is? How can she not fall to her knees and hold him next to her chest forever?

BROKEN BONES

THE FORGED steel teeth on the yellow ripper bucket of the backhoe scoops several yards deeper than the church father had done with his small spade. The bucket scoops all the way down to the anklebones looped in fabric that once belonged to the girl with the eyes like sky. The one who had seen the gray one fall. The laughing then crying one who had made the journey south from the great hot basin and founded this settlement next to the cold flooding river.

THE LAST HOPE FOR DORIS DAY

Chance has spent all morning glancing through Doris Day's front window hoping she'll flash him the smile that has given him a reason to go on in this world. When the boss sends him to paint the back of the house, and he realizes he has a view of a bedroom, he blushes and thinks about her in all those movies. He doesn't want to see her. Not her, not like that.

So he stays focused on the wall he's painting. Every once in a while, he thinks he sees something moving, but he doesn't look. It'd be like leering at his sister.

After a half an hour of this particular brand of torture, someone calls out, "Are you Chance?"

"Sure," he says. It's a man in a gray suit and sunglasses, walking across the lawn. Young guy, maybe thirty or so.

"Your boss told me you know about bomb shelters."

The boss always does this to him because Chance was there when the nukes went off. He fought in Japan, and then they sent him to Nevada to build Anytown, U.S.A. in the middle of the desert just so they could watch it evaporate in atomic holocaust. He and his buddies constructed it and drove forty miles away to hide behind rocks when the big one went off. Then the doctors lined them up half-naked and checked them out to see if they were going to die from the radiation. So far, he hasn't.

Chance spends a lot of his day thinking about the towns he built and what Nagasaki and its people looked like afterward. He thinks about the kid he was in his first year of business college when he dropped out and signed up to protect America and Doris Day from evil.

"Yeah, you can tell Miss Day that living like this right in Los

Angeles, she's going to need one if she wants to make it through the next war." In the last ten jobs they've had, the boss has had Chance upsell seven clients bomb shelters. Each time, the boss has bought Chance a good bottle of booze, which Chance always passes on to his priest. Last time, the boss talked about maybe bringing Chance in on sales, promoting him.

"Miss Day?"

"You don't work for her?"

He shakes his head in a no. "Her husband, Mr. Melcher. I'm his assistant."

Somehow the idea of her with a husband makes him sad.

"You think I can talk to him?"

The assistant glances at his gold-looking watch. "Nah, he's probably left. Anyway, he told me to take care of it. What are we looking at here?"

"You mean like price?" The assistant nods, but Chance isn't ready to talk money yet. "Depends on what you want. You figure if the Soviets are going to drop the big one, this is the third or fourth city they'll take out. First D.C., then New York, and then either here or Chicago."

It's hard to tell if he's got the assistant or not with the man's sunglasses on. "Okay," he says.

"You wouldn't believe the kinds of things I saw in Nagasaki. I mean, you wouldn't believe it."

He takes off his glasses, and Chance gets that little look of human concern. He's got the man thinking. "Yeah?"

"Women with their skin boiled off. Children wandering around looking for their parents. Not a lot of men. They were all off fighting in the war. The old people were the worst, just kind of hobbling around. Some of them were burned everywhere, waiting to die and hoping it'd happen soon."

There was another thing that Chance never tries to describe or name. The people he saw were missing something behind their eyes. He knows what it was, part of it at least. They'd lost the war and their towns, but more than that, they saw everything end in a flash, their whole world ceased to exist. He'd seen soldiers who'd been through slaughterhouse battles, and they never had that empty lost look. Not like those people.

"You don't want Miss Day or Mr. Melcher to have to live like them."

"No."

"Building a shelter is a way to have hope."

The people who hadn't been burned seemed as empty and lost as those who'd nearly died, and Chance and his buddies said over and over that if they saw the nukes coming they'd run toward them instead of trying to hide. Better to be dead than alive in that world.

"After the war, we tested out bomb shelters during real live nuclear explosions out in the desert. I promise you that you want at least ten feet of dirt between you and the world above."

Chance can see by this assistant's eyes that he can set his price now if he wants to. "I promise you this too. We can build her a shelter she can live in for one thousand dollars, but if she is going to really thrive, you're going to want to spend at least five thousand."

The assistant nods and puts on his serious face. "What does Mr. Melcher get for that?" he asks, but his mind is already made up. Chance goes through the specs, talks about the design and the sizes. He tells him about bathrooms and food storage and concrete lining, but all of this is memorized and his mind wanders.

He's never built a shelter for himself or anyone he loves, and he wouldn't. This job where he's moving up in the world is built on a lie. He thinks of Doris Day wandering around in the apocalypse that was Nagasaki. He is giving her that life right now, and this afternoon, he will tell the bossman that they could start an entire side business selling these shelters. They could post a couple of ads in the newspaper that play on fear and hope, and they'll have all the work they need. He knows he's going to do that because it's so easy, and people are scared but about all the wrong things.

As he talks, he sees movement out of the corner of his eye. It's the woman herself. He thinks it is. She's blond, but her back's to him. The way she's moving it looks like she's singing. In her left hand, she's holding a martini glass and a cigarette as naturally as if she has been doing it her whole life. She takes a sip, and then she twirls, and he almost catches her face for a brief second of what he imagines as ecstatic joy.

The assistant frowns at him, and Chance wonders if he lost a sale because the guy thinks he's a pervert. He hopes he has. He hopes that the Soviets get smart and blow them up right now. He prays that they snap off the world before she has the chance to know that this life isn't about joy, and it has never been about hope.

WHEN RACHEL SLEEPS

When Rachel sleeps stretched across the entire backseat of the car, she dreams of the tattoo on her father's arm, the numbers in their neat row that she has seen only once. He always wears long sleeves, even on hot days, even here in the Miracle Mile. When she sleeps, she goes to that secret place where her father says her brother and grandparents are waiting for her. She dreams of her real name, the one that changed when they moved to this country. She wakes up when the car stops. Her father gathers her up in his arms, and she smiles to herself that she is a part of this family that keeps so many things unseen. It's like she's special. It's like she knows where the magician has hidden the dove.

CHILDREN LET YOUR VOICES SING HIGHER THAN THE EXPLOSIONS

THE MORNING that she read "Harlem" by Langston Hughes to her 9th grade English class was the first time a student made her cry out of cruelty. It had been the one boy in class she hadn't been able to reach, who bragged he was going to play alongside of Michael Jordan and who bet his coach $1000 that he would be signed to the NBA, that school was a waste of his time. The same one who called her a stupid bitch.

She hadn't allowed him the satisfaction of crying in his presence, but she carried the sting of his words home with her, his mocking of her flaring nostrils as she read the line: "*Or does it explode?*" Coincidentally, the second time she cried in the classroom was in front of his younger sister—in front of the whole class, in fact—although two years later and for a much different reason. She had wheeled in the AV cart with the TV so the class could watch Nelson Mandela's inauguration. The newscaster explained how, under apartheid rule, Mandela had served 27 years in a jail on Robben Island for attempting to overthrow the apartheid state. That after being released and subsequently elected as the first non-white head of state in South African history, Mandela personally invited his jailer to stand next to him during his inaugural ceremony as an act of healing. As he stepped outside of his cell, he said, he knew that if he didn't leave his bitterness and hatred there behind him on the island, he would never be free. That he could achieve more through mercy than retribution.

Three years after that she cried in class for a third time, on a morning she had planned to read that same Hughes poem about what happens to a dream deferred, but just minutes before she had been called in by the new principal and told that the promotion she had been promised had been given instead to the new football coach who had just transferred in from another school in the district, but that she was highly valued asset. Very highly valued. And he thanked her for all she did. Then, that she should try not to take these things so personally, that she should actually be thanking him since he had protected her from a much harder job, not really suited for emotional types, and now all she had to worry about was keeping her class looking nice for open house next week, which shouldn't be too hard for a pretty gal like herself. Then, he called her "sweetie" and tried to hug her, but she slipped away and out the door and in those echoing steps down the hallway back to her classroom, she changed lesson plans, instead dimming the lights and starting a video, rolling her chair to the back wall so they could not see her shaking.

That same week, the student who was the first to make her cry seven years earlier by mocking her and calling her a bitch, swung a baseball bat at the head of a USC freshman just to take his new Nikes.

That freshman, sprawled lifeless with one bare foot and the other sock pulled halfway off, just three months earlier while walking down Martin Luther King Boulevard to pick up his youngest sister from school, stopped when the police jumped out of their car, shouting at him to show them his hands. He had, but they rushed up and spun him around and pinned him against a wall, the bricks splitting his eyebrow.

From a passing bus, the new refugee from Nicaragua who was riding to her second job of the day, witnessed his head hitting the brick, and she slapped the glass with her palms in four quick blows trying to get them to stop, but she went unnoticed amid the shouts and the bus engine's rumble as the light turned green, and she rolled away from the scene.

The muscular forearm that lifted the boy off the ground in a chokehold was the same arm that had dropped two other boys from his neighborhood, putting one into a coma. The same arm that would hold a stiff salute as medals were pinned on him by his superiors at his retirement, honoring his selfless service to the community as an officer of the peace.

The forensic detective who linked the blood on the Nikes to the murder, when she heard the perp lived with his girlfriend and a newborn baby daughter, stayed well past the end of her shift to follow the arresting officer to the apartment, and after the arrest accompanied protective services and then sat with the mother and son, offering comfort. Over the years she visited often, and checked in on them when they moved, and eventually attended the daughter's high school graduation—from the same school her dad had dropped out of.

Today in that same classroom, a new English teacher reads aloud a poem by Wisława Szymborska, the one with the line about apologizing to time for all in the world that is overlooked each second, and that poem would make a freshman want to become an English teacher herself. And later the class would read the new teacher's favorite short story—the one about a group of strangers jolted to a stop in a dark elevator in San Francisco in a building just rocked by the Loma Prieta earthquake, and how the little girl clinging to her doll had started to cry, and how the soft singing from her mother calmed all riders there, until one by one they spontaneously started to join in, a choir that lifted away their fear, and even though no one could remember what anyone else looked like before the lights went out, they all knew they were one family in that place, creating a joyous noise against the darkness.

Tonight, on the dimly lit top floor of the building that was called the Library Tower when it was first built, the one with lights like a chevron crown on a giant chess piece queen, the maid from Nicaragua pushes a vacuum cleaner across the gold carpeting of the bank executive's empty office. And when she is done, before leaving and closing the door to the highest place she will ever be, she pauses to stare out at the city spread beneath her like a promise. The way it flashes and shimmers reminds her of the river back home. And she starts to hum along with the song streaming from the cassette boombox on her cart, the song whose story was penned by a man of her village as a poem, then turned into song by his friend. The true story told by the once-tortured prisoner himself, the one who sat bound and hooded for nearly a year, beaten daily, but hurt more by the memories of what the foreign government-backed soldiers had done to his friends and his family—forcing them to watch as their mothers and daughters were raped and cut away piece by piece, their fathers and brothers skinned alive. And he sat up and vowed his revenge straight into the face of his torturer, and upon his release when he became a Minister of the new ruling party, he made it a point to find out where his torturer sat in a cell, defeated, and he went there and unlocked the door and smiled at him, proclaiming that his hour of revenge had finally come as he promised it would. He looked his torturer in the eye and told him that his punishment was to be this: that he and his new government would do him no harm, and would do his children no harm, and in that way would show the country who they were—and the maid shakes her head, her eyes filling, *Dios mio*—that his personal revenge would be the right of their children to the schools, and to the flowers—and she thinks of the flowers back home when she was a girl, so different from her new home of *Los Angeles*, now trembling, and how afraid she was when she first crossed the border and the coyotes took from her all they could—and she sings a bit louder, the line about the good there in the eyes of the people—*sí*—and then she thinks of the boy whose head met the brick that day and the blood and the people oppressed, the people, the people—yes, she sobs—and she sings when you who use your hands to torture can no longer look up…—she closes her eyes—then my personal revenge will be to offer to you these hands that once you so mistreated—*sí*—but how you will never take away their tenderness.

E PLURIBUS UNUM

WHEN HILDA lays her head down she hears her heart pulse against the pillow. Sometimes it calms her. Sometimes it beats away all other thought, and then she can't sleep and has to shift her head, and if that doesn't work, roll over to sleep on her other side. On the evenings of the days she spends out in nature, doing her field research, the sound of her heartbeat in her ear against the pillow calms and soothes her before it fades and disappears into sleep, the top of a stone sinking in water.

At Big Rock Creek her eye catches a beautiful specimen. It takes her breath. She always has a tinge of regret when she removes a thing from its natural place. *Leave only footprints and take only memories*, as she tells her students. But that weighs against her utilitarian tendencies to make decisions based on the greater good. Better to remove one small thing from its natural state if it helps overall. Yes, pragmatic compromise. But the same argument was used to bus school children, and that wasn't fair. Quotas. Like in the Science Department. Band-aid adjustments instead of larger solutions. Meanwhile, the daily struggles, moment by moment. She turns the rock over in her hands, admiring the beauty on all sides of it.

To remove one small thing from where it naturally occurs, naturally belongs perhaps, and seen by one person every week maybe, surrounded by countless others similar ones so hardly a one-of-a-kind object, and to repurpose it as a tool to educate hundreds at a time, well, what's wrong with that? She pauses. But by that same logic, zoos. And circuses, disingenuously disguising profit motive. Picassos in private parlors. What's different with you, Hilda, she asks herself. She raises her eyebrows, then frowns slightly. Does she profit from taking a stone from the wilderness?

Yes, personally. It gives her great pleasure, and so she keeps it in her house when not teaching that unit. Is that selfish? Beyond its service to education once per semester when she takes it to class to cover that unit, the assumed privilege of possession, claiming souvenirs from nature to display in her own home. Her own zoo? Bookshelf as cage. *Oh dear, no.* She plays out the pros and cons of her actions constantly in her head. As one who wants to do good. Be good. She struggles so with answers. Always questions.

Hilda finds it ironic that she spends more time teaching differences when all of life is 99.9% similar and 100% interrelated, she tells her colleagues. If we all focused on that, people would behave better. But they have to be shown, her friend reminds. But survival, the Dean says condescendingly, showing the unscuffed soles of his shoes as he props his crossed legs on his desk, relies on power differences, predator and prey. We are not equal. Survival relies on respecting that and protecting family, so we should not trust others, should resist outsiders for the threats they truly are, look out for number one. He doesn't like Hilda much, for some reason. Maybe because she is smarter than he is, and he knows it. Or maybe it is just that he doesn't like smart women in general. Or maybe he doesn't like women at all. He certainly didn't like the story she told him of the two women who built and cohabited the house she purchased in the Mojave foothills after they died.

Lynn and Nancy lived together for sixty years, kept goats and trained horses, bred and sold burros and earned good money, loved each other madly and died happy, one week apart. The Dean had reacted with a grimace and said it wasn't natural. He also often quoted from Ayn Rand and insisted that empathy was not a natural state, a real threat to survival of the strongest, in fact, which is the way of nature. Civilization is a man-made survival mechanism, he admitted, but arguably a band-aid too. Every man for himself. Hilda hated his way of looking at the world. But it's a losing end game if you listen only to your own heartbeat, Hilda had offered, because we are all cohabiting here. She thinks of this as she turns the rock over again, dragging her fingertips across the darker underside where it had been sitting.

When hiking in higher elevations, Hilda sometimes lays her head down on the bank of the river, as close to the water's edge as possible, presses her ear to the ground and looks out at the current. Especially after heavy rains, she is able to see the "Thread of the Current"—the middle of the river flowing higher than its edges. As the river slows from the friction of its banks, slows from bottom impediments, slows at the surface from air and wind, a faster river-within-the-river forced by snowmelt or runoff rips beneath the surface, lifting a bulge as it rushes by less impeded through its own center. The faster and larger the flowing thread, the higher the bulge. So odd and thrilling to see a river rising at its core like that, defying gravity, like a rib cage swelled upon full inhale. There, with her ear to the ground at the river's edge, Hilda inhales as her yoga instructor has taught her, filling the lungs as much as possible—in, in, in—listening for her own airways singing as her tissue slows the flow of the sky through her. As she exhales she begins to notice her own rushing heartbeat at her core from her direct connection with planet, imagines it as the heartbeat of the Earth herself pulsing through her, imagines this as an ideal state for any creature to exist in, listening closely, awake and aware, connected with all it touches and what flows through it—air, food, unseen waves of energy. As one likewise flows through nature the same, as her yoga instructor says.

Hilda closes her eyes and feels at peace. Then bliss. She sees, as if projected, a cobalt blue that transitions to a deeper violet, a swirling of amber at the edges then like a third eye—or is it a lighter halo surrounding a black pinpoint pupil-like core? Then all sound stops, and she is in some other state. Thinking back on it, it was like the pause and silence of the blank page at the end of a poem. When she gets home she writes quickly in her journal and finishes the sonnet she had begun a month ago. Then she takes the specimen from her bag and places it on the window sill so that it sits half exposed to the direct noonday sunlight, half in the shade of the window casing. She considers the rock as a guest, existing now as half-domesticated, half-wild. She plans on returning it, some day, to the place she picked it up, or as close to it as possible based on the notes she carefully recorded in her journal as she removed it.

That evening she sketches it with both 4H hard and 6B black charcoal pencils, adds highlights with a stick of white Conté. She will use homemade paints made from pigments of beet root, blueberries, turmeric, mustard, cornflower, cinnamon and blood, mixed with binders of gum arabic, egg white and spit. Parts of herself mixed literally into her art. She likes that.

After a week of admiring the specimen, she decides that if she had a favorite rock, this would be it. It is a "DETRITAL SEDIMENTARY ROCK"—as she writes in block letters beneath her rendering of it. A conglomerate, with fragments of many different clasts, or rock fragments, broken away from larger stones and boulders, each weathered by water, ice, wind—each tumbled separately through gravity and river to assemble into this singular, beautiful thing. Rocks eroded smaller and smaller by classification: from boulder to cobble to pebble to granule to sand to silt to clay, finer and finer each step of the way in sedimentary successions. Such sediments when hardened together make sedimentary rocks, she tells her students, from the finest flour-like clay-sized bits that make up shale that crumbles in your fist like beach cliffs, to grittier siltstone made of silt, but without shale's visible layers. To larger, porous, water-permeable sandstone, that you see used in filtration systems. Rocks assembled from detrital sediments of pebbles or larger clasts are called conglomerates, she explains, and can be composed of rounded grains smoothed by water, as when tumbled down a river, say, or angular broken breccia chipped by rockslides down a mountain.

This rock in her illustration is from the San Gabriel Mountains, found at the bottom of Big Rock Creek, which heads at Vincent Gap near Fenner Canyon and flows some 11 miles in all, first northwest past Dorr Canyon, Sycamore Flat, Holcomb Canyon, Punchbowl Canyon with the tiered Devil's Punchbowl to the west, then turns south past Shoemaker Canyon and Big Rock Springs where it enters the Mojave Desert, crosses Fort Tejon Road and fans out to become Big Rock Wash—she points to the places on the map as she lectures. This is a conglomerate of lithic fragments, or particles of recognizable rock—smooth rounded pebbles of various colors of brown, red, white, blue and green—all cemented naturally by monomineralic fragments, or mineral grains—the larger new bound by older and finer clay to become this very rock.

Silly to think she has a favorite rock, but she does now, especially after having studied it and painted it and taught it. Yes, mainly because it is beautiful beyond what words or lead or paint can convey. But also, she thinks, because it is clastic—rocks composed of broken pieces of older rocks, and the most common rock found on the face of the earth. She loves that, and loves how each thing residing within it is a broken individual from a larger source, all relocated, all pulled down and smoothed by natural forces, each arriving separately to the same place, each thing becoming bound with the others by the finest essence of what came before, all co-existing now as one thing. This is the story of us, Hilda thinks, as she smudges the hard lines of her new sketch softer with her thumb. This is California.

NOTES

THE AUTHORS would like to thank Mark Givens and Pelekinesis Press for offering a home to this non-traditional work, and for supporting writers and all genres of new writing with grace and good will.

Also, to D. J. Waldie. First, for his life of important scholarship and writing, especially the genre-defying art that is *Holy Land: A Suburban Memoir*. Second, for his generosity in penning the insightful introduction to this genre-challenged book, thereby elevating our efforts beyond measure. Likewise, to Robert Petersen. First, for his important contributions to education and culture, especially through his work on KCET's Departures. Second, for allowing us to use some of that work—an excerpt from "California, Calafia, Khalif: The Origin of the Name 'California'"—as the epigraph to this book.

Also to CSULB's MFA programs in Creative Writing in Poetry and Fiction, of which the authors of this book are alumni, and to the brilliant mentors there—particularly Gerald Locklin, Charles Harper Webb, Ray Zepeda, Suzanne Greenberg, and Robert J. Brophy.

Also to Laguna College of Art and Design and Mt. San Antonio College, which foster environments of creative thinking and which have long supported the authors' work.

Grant and John would like to especially thank the City of Anaheim and the Sequoia and Kings Canyon National Parks for appointing us as Poets Laureate of those places, respectively, thereby providing us a larger platform to promote the values at the heart of this book via our roles as literary ambassadors for our local communities.

Lastly, to our friends, family, students, and colleagues.

The authors are donating their earnings from this book to not-for-profit organizations whose work is the same as the goals of this writing: equal opportunities for everyone to have their voices heard and an equal place at the table; a broader and deeper understanding of what has come before us; and a more inclusive and respectful community in the here and now, for all living things who share this place and time in the continuum.

ACKNOWLEDGMENTS

Thanks to the editors of the following publications for being the first to bring these stories to a wider audience:

"1850." *Manifest West.*

"All of Those Boys Are Dead Now." *Broad River Review.*

"Art in the West." *Linden Avenue Review.*

"The California Water War." *Tahoma Literary Review* and *Best Small Fiction Anthology.*

"The Golden Gate Bridge." *Avalon Literary Journal.*

"In the Tule Fog." *The Nashwaak Review.*

"Nathaniel." *The Storyteller.*

"The Savior." *The MacGuffin.*

"The Sorrowful Music of Cows." *Shadowgraph Online Quarterly.*

"The View from the Monkey Bars." *In Parenthesis.*

"The Water Hunter." *Verdad.*

"When Rachel Sleeps." *Winamop.*

The title "Children let your voices sing higher than the explosions" refers to a line in the poem "That Country" by Grace Paley.

The Wisława Szymborska poem alluded to in that same story is "Under One Small Star."

The excerpt from "Darktown Strutters' Ball" by Shelton Brooks was published in 1917.

The lyrics alluded to later in that same story are from the song "Mi Venganza Personal" ("My Personal Revenge") by Tomás Borge and Luis Enrique Mejía Godoy.

This book uses the font Minion Pro, a typeface inspired by calligraphy and late Renaissance type, with large apertures for readability, humanist axis tilt, flowing adnate serifs, elegant long descenders, and fine details that echo natural pen strokes. The section font is called Seaside Resort, designed by Nick Curtis, and the title font is called Avenir, designed by Adrian Frutiger in 1988.

If you would like to use this book for educational purposes, discounted copies can be acquired through the publisher at www.pelekinesis.com

GRANT HIER

Grant Hier is the inaugural Poet Laureate of Anaheim. His long poem, *Untended Garden: Histories and Reinhabitation in Suburbia*, was awarded Prize Americana in 2014 and published as a book by Poetry Press the following year. It was subsequently nominated for both an American Book Award and the Kate Tufts Discovery Award. Two poetry collections, *The Difference Between* and *Similitude*, were published in 2018 (both on Pelekinesis). Grant was previously awarded the Nancy Dew Taylor Prize for Literary Excellence in Poetry and the Kick Prize for poetry, and he is the poetry editor for *Chiron Review*. His writing has been anthologized in such books as *Only Light Can Do That* (Rattling Wall/PEN Center USA), *Monster Verse—Human and Inhuman Poems* (Knopf/Everyman), *Orange County: A Literary Field Guide* (Heyday), *LA Fiction Anthology* (Red Hen), and *John Fante: A Critical Gathering* (Fairleigh Dickinson University Press). He is the writer and producer on the CD, *Joyride: Friends Take the Wheel*, a compilation of performances of the words and music of Louie Pérez by various artist. In addition to writing, Grant is a musical artist, visual artist, and former graphic designer and art director (he co-art-directed the cover of *Joyride* with Louie Pérez). As a voice actor, he contributed to the audio book of George Saunders' *Lincoln in the Bardo*, which won the 2018 Audie Award for Audiobook of the year. Grant is a Full Professor at Laguna College of Art and Design where he teaches a variety of Liberal Arts classes, including creative writing. More at www.granthier.com

JOHN BRANTINGHAM

John Brantingham is he first poet laureate of Sequoia and Kings Canyon National Park, a writer, and a professor at Mt. San Antonio College, where he is director of the Creative Writing program. His work has been published in hundreds of magazines in the United States and United Kingdom. His story was featured in *The Best Small Fictions 2016*. He has also been featured on *Writer's Almanac* and other radio programs, and his poem "Home Techtonics" was used for the Regents Exam in 2012 taken by all college-bound New York high school students. He has been nominated for multiple Pushcart Prizes and won Pearl Magazine's Fiction contest. His chapbooks include *Putting in a Window* (Finishing Line Press), *The Mediterranean Garden* (Finishing Line Press), and *Heroes for Today* (Pudding House Press). His books include *The Gift of Form* (Spout Hill Press), *East of Los Angeles* (Anaphora Press), *Mann of War* (Oak Tree Press), *Let Us All Pray Now to Our Own Strange Gods* (World Parade Books), *The Green of Sunset* (Moon Tide Press), *LA Fiction Anthology* (Red H en Press), *Dual Impression: Poetic Conversations about Art* with Jeffrey Graessley (Silver Birch Press), and *A Sublime and Tragic Dance* with Kendall Johnson (Cholla Needles Press).

He is the president of the San Gabriel Valley Literary Festival and was a fiction editor for *Chiron Review*. He has taught for the Northwestern Institute for the Literary Art's low-residence MFA program.

INDEX

Age of the Mastodons 179
Aguirre, Sheriff Martin G. 23–32
Artistic Expression 50, 237
Bachelard, Gaston 16–17
Border and Border Crossing 44, 46, 53–55, 59–61, 66–67, 226–227
Brick 17, 39–43
California
   Geology 45
   Naming of 13–14
   Statehood 44
California Water War 191–192, 194–195
Civil Uprisings / Riots. *See also* Denny, Reginald
   Rodney King 17, 39–43, 77–78, 90–95
   Zoot Suit 81
Concentration Camps 236
Crime and Punishment 98–100, 104–105
de Certeau, Michel 17
de Montalvo, Garcia Ordonez 13–14
Denny, Reginald 17, 39–43
Didion, Joan 19
Domestic Violence 56–58, 136
Donner Pass 16
Dream Deferred 42, 237–240
Drought 129–131, 176–178, 191–192, 194–195
Earthquake 196–200, 202–204
Fire 137–140, 207–212
Floods 24–25, 52

Freedom from Racism 44, 82–85
Geologic Past 45
Geronimo 21–32
Hollywood and the Idea of Fame 116–121, 124–125
Homelessness 110, 132–135, 157–175
Housing Crisis 106–109, 111–115
Human Trafficking / Sex Slavery 122, 123
Internment Camps 82–85, 228–229. *See also* Concentration Camps
Khalif / Khalifa 13–14
Long Beach, California 51, 86–88, 90–93, 122
The Los Angeles Herald 24
Mammoths 179
Migration 13–14, 21, 44, 46, 49, 50, 59–61, 82–85, 136
Movie Industry 116–121, 124
Mumford, Lewis 19
Native Americans 25, 47, 49, 52, 179, 193, 201, 213, 231
The Natural World
   Competing Edenic Visions of California
      Constructed (William Mulholland's Vision) 147–148, 157–175, 176–178, 217–220, 221–225, 230, 232–235, 241–245
      Unconstructed (John Muir's Vision) 89, 141, 142–144, 205–206, 207–212
   Deserts 53–55, 191–192
   Forests 89, 141, 142–144, 145–146, 157–175, 180–190
   Waterways 176–178, 191–192, 194–195, 201, 202–204
Need for Economic Security 59–64, 97, 101, 129–131
Nuclear Dread 217–220, 221–225, 230, 232–235
O'Connor, Flannery 17
People's Relationship to Nature 89, 141, 142–144, 145–146, 147–148, 149–153, 157–175, 176–178, 180–190, 191–192, 194–195, 205–206, 241–245
Pomona, California 97
Prison 98–100
Sequoia and Kings Canyon National Parks 89, 141, 142–144
Spanish Invasion of California 13–14

Steinbeck, John 33–35
Stewart, Kathleen 18
Union Station 102–103
Unrealistic Dreams
   Fleeing War and Terror 53–55, 66–67, 136
War 56–58, 65, 66–67, 68–76, 79, 80, 86–88, 129–131

www.ingramcontent.com/pod-product-compliance
Lightning Source LLC
Chambersburg PA
CBHW031315160426
43196CB00007B/545